THE LITTLE
BOOK OF MICK

THE LITTLE BOOK OF MICK

PAUL KILDUFF

Gill & Macmillan

Gill & Macmillan Ltd
Hume Avenue, Park West, Dublin 12
with associated companies throughout the world
www.gillmacmillan.ie

© Paul Kilduff 2008
978 07171 4492 1

Typography design by Make Communication
Print origination by Carole Lynch
Printed in the UK by CPI Bookmarque, Croydon, CR0 4TD

This book is typeset in Linotype Minion and Neue Helvetica.

The paper used in this book comes from the wood pulp of
managed forests. For every tree felled, at least one tree is
planted, thereby renewing natural resources.

A CIP catalogue record for this book is available
from the British Library.

5 4 3 2 1

CONTENTS

FLYING

'The wings fall off all the time. There's too many discounts.'

'Are we are trying to blow up the notion that flying is some kind of orgasmic experience rather than a glorified bus service? Yes, we are. An airplane is nothing more than a bus with wings on.'

'I think we certainly have democratised flight, in that there's no curtains anymore, there's no business class anymore, you're not made to feel, you know, two inches tall, like, "Here you go, down with the poor people at the back." Everybody is the same on Ryanair.'

'The problem with the airline industry is it is so populated with people who grew up in the 1940s or 1950s who got their excitement looking at airplanes flying over-head. They wanted to be close to airplanes. Mercifully I was a child of the 1960s and a trained accountant, so aircraft don't do anything for me.'

'There's a lot of big egos in this industry. That might be a better title for them, including myself, rather than entrepreneurs. Most chief executives got into this business because they want to travel for a living. Not me, I want to work.'

'It's a stupid business which generally loses a lot of money. With the exception of Southwest and ourselves, and easyJet to a lesser extent, nobody makes a lot of money at it.'

'We'll double the size we are now, unless we do something stupid like have a crash or join an alliance. There's a challenge every day in the airline industry not to do something stupid. Airlines are characterised by people who do something stupid.'

'In any airline there is always a strong possibility of management stupidity. The biggest threat we face is a management fuck-up, and getting fat and dumb and happy for a couple of years.'

'It doesn't matter how good you think you are in the airline business. We live every hour of every day with "How do we avoid ever having an accident?" I never want to have an accident on my conscience. I think any airline that has a crash will suffer a disproportionate effect. Every airline is only as good as its safety record. I am not going to defend our safety because that is almost like denying you beat your wife. There is no safer airline in Europe than Ryanair. We have had no major incidents in 18 years. Everywhere, safety is always the number one priority. The notion that any airline would be going around compromising on safety is just crazy.'

'Every year seems to be an awful year for the airline industry, at least according to our high-fare competitors.

If only there hadn't been a war in Iraq, if only SARS hadn't broken out in the Far East, if only 9/11 hadn't happened, if only foot-and-mouth hadn't broken out, but for the fuel shocks, etc; the list goes on and on. It seems that losing money in the airline business is always a 'surprise', always somebody else's fault, and always due to external factors beyond management's control.'

'The airline industry is going to suffer a downturn. Every six to seven years, the backside falls out of it, we've had six years of record profits, so we are due one in the next three to six months. Historically, the downturns have usually come after British Airways and Aer Lingus order new jets, which they have both just done, so we're battening down the hatches in readiness for the shit to hit the fan.'

On travel agents: 'Screw the travel agents. Take the fuckers out and shoot them. They are a waste of bloody time. What have they done for passengers over the years? I certainly won't be going to Cairo for the Association of British Travel Agents convention. I can think of no more useless a convention. It's a bit like holding a meeting of Alcoholics Anonymous in a big pub. We prefer to avoid the talking shops. We're too busy carrying passengers at lower fares.'

On meeting with the Irish Travel Agents' Association: 'We told them to go to hell.'

'We may not be even flying in 2030. We may be all beamed about like Star Trek.'

LOW FARES

'For years flying has been the preserve of rich fuckers. Now everyone can afford to fly.'

'Everyone always says, "What's your secret?" It's very simple. Our strategy is like Wal-Mart and Dell. We pile it high and sell it cheap. If anyone beats us on price, we will lower ours. We are the Tesco of the airline industry. We took the supermarket concept to the skies. Even the unemployed can afford to fly Ryanair.'

'The low-cost model only really works for short-haul flights. If we started flying farther afield, we'd have to do something stupid, like introducing what I call a "rich class" to make it pay.'

'What the hell have we been doing for the last fifty years? We've been gouging the consumer, and putting the cost of air travel beyond the means of 80% or 90% of the travelling public. The lowest fare between Dublin and London in 1985, before Ryanair started flying, was £130. It had to be booked four weeks in advance and it was non-changeable and non-refundable.'

'The alternative to progress is Thomas Hardy's Wessex: horse-drawn carts, people living below the poverty line and only the very rich going abroad on Italian tours. Now we make it possible for everybody to go on Italian tours. The car was only liberating in the 1950s for the 5% who could afford them. Nobody moved more than three miles from where they were born. Growing up in Ireland in the 1960s, flying abroad was a dream. Young people now want to go to Ibiza on bonking holidays. Let them. Ask them in downtown Afghanistan if they would like the M25 and they would bite your hand off.'

'We're the most profitable airline in the world. We don't do anything that loses money. We don't fly a load of people for £1.99. We might fly 50% of them on a Tuesday in November at £1.99, as it's better than having 50 empty seats. And 25 will buy coffee, 10 a sandwich, one will rent a car. I will make money out of that stuff. We'll take anything to fill flights.'

'We are in the middle of a war on Iraq. Our fares are dumped down on the floor. We are charging fares of €1, €5 and €9, yet taxes, charges and fees are €12 and €13 on top of that, but that is what I have to do. The point was made that this fare is higher than my costs. It is not, it is much lower than my costs. I am losing money on a shed load of seats I am selling at the moment, but at least I am selling the seats.'

'Fares of one cent or one penny are much too low, but if that is what we have to do to fill our aircraft, then that's what we have to do. It is our intention to charge even lower fares, or rather offer more seats available at these ridiculously low prices, because that is what our customers want.'

'I cannot make money by selling all seats at €1. My average fare must be approximately €43. However, I sell 40% of seats each year at the lowest fare, which is always substantially lower than €43. Nevertheless, given all the income generated, I can make money.'

'It is like some Russian analysis, like the five-year plan. You pay for what you get. I will sell you a seat today on an aircraft going to London tomorrow. There will be passengers on board that aircraft tomorrow who will have paid me €1 and there will be passengers who will have paid me—probably at the top end—€129 or €149. They have each paid for what they got.'

'As long as it leads to lower fares for Mr and Mrs Joe Public, we think that's good news.'

'Are Ryanair's fares fair? Yes. There is only one test and that is whether consumers support what we do. We are usually the first to come forward with a new policy. We are not taking unaccompanied minors because we cannot handle them. We do not give back refunds or taxes, we keep the whole lot if there is a "no show". The test of something being fair is whether consumers support it. We have the support of many consumers. We will take all the brickbats we get from the press or anybody else because the competition does not like us. The acid test will be when passenger traffic will be up on the previous month.'

'We have no plans to fly at night. Firstly, our aircraft are in the air from 6.30 a.m. to 11 p.m. at night, they fly on average eight flights per day, that's two sectors of four flights each, and we change the crews after a sector. More importantly we need the aircraft to be maintained during the night-time and safety is our top priority. Not so recently people had to fly on charter flights at night-time to get cheap fares. Now with our airline you can get cheap fares all day long. And there's no fare cheaper than a free fare.'

'If somebody comes up with a lower fare than us on any route then we will drop our fare straight away. We are the only airline that offers that kind of commitment. If there's a fare war, we'll start it and we'll finish it.'

'It's never going to be cheaper to fly across Europe than this summer and winter. I like it when customers win and our competitors lose. We have never yet lost money by reducing fares to the travelling public. I think at the moment we have more cash than British Airways or Lufthansa.'

'If someone wants a fare war they are going to get it. If any of you lads out there think you are going to make money, well, we are coming after you.'

'I see no reason why fares don't keep falling for 10 years. I don't see why in 10 years' time you wouldn't fly people for free. More than half of our passengers will fly free. Why don't airports pay us for delivering the passengers to their shops?'

'We gave away 15% of our seats last year for free. If we didn't give them away, they'd be empty. There is no reason why we should have to charge fares. If we make enough money from other services and keep our costs down, we will make flights free. I'm working on a multiplex model. They make most of their money from the sale of popcorn, drinks and sweets, not from cinema tickets.'

'If we can increase the average ancillary spend per passenger by enough, then we could afford to cut fares to zero. Ultimately we are trying to get to a situation where we can give away tickets, not on Monday morning or peak times, but on midweek seats. All other airlines are asking how they can get up fares, we are asking how can we get rid of them.'

'I have a vision in the future that we will be flying everyone for free, but I'm damned if I'm going to pay for them to fly.'

'We're so crazy, we'll pay people to fly with us. I can imagine the diary writers saying Ryanair must be desperate.'

'We succeed because we offer the lower fares that customers want.'

'Price is the best form of loyalty. Ryanair owns price.'

If you can't find a low fare on Ryanair: 'You're a moron.'

PASSENGERS

'We do not take money. Passengers give it to us voluntarily. This could not be any clearer.'

*O*n allegations of flying lager louts on stag weekends: 'We call them the Chianti louts heading to villas in Tuscany and the South of France. We expect the Chianti louts, the lager louts and anybody who just wants a stunningly low fare to buy our tickets.'

'If the worst the locals can complain about is a couple of hen or stag parties, how bad is it? We'd like a lot of ballet-loving opera-attending visitors.'

'Our most frequent fliers would be what you'd call upper-class, the very rich. Our most frequent fliers during the summer are people who have large holiday homes in Malaga, Marbella, south of France, Italy, you name it, sending the kids, nannies, gardeners, wives, girlfriends, mistresses up and down on our flights.'

On Irish passengers flying to Poland to buy overseas property: 'The flights are our oddest mix of passengers, full of Polish construction workers coming here and Irish heading off to invest in the next new property thing. They should be selling to the people there, not buying from them. Remember Joe Kennedy's advice before the 1929 crash—sell when the shoe shine boy is buying.'

'I would be mystified if anyone is buying a property in France or Spain on the basis that Ryanair gives them a lifetime guarantee of cheap fares. We don't have any obligation to second-home-owners that we are always going to carry you there for ever and a day. It's called caveat emptor. Please don't ask me to feel sorry for rich people with second homes in France. I'd far rather feel sorry for ordinary people in the UK who can't afford to fly with British Airways' high fares.'

'When we used Jet-Way airbridges, we found that they were the fourth largest cause of delays. Either the Jet-way wasn't there when we arrived, or the buffoon who was driving it was out by a few inches, and had to take the whole thing back and forth again before landing up at our doors. If it's raining, passengers will just walk a little faster.'

'We should outlaw business class traffic. We should pack them into economy class rather than have the fat and overpaid flying around on flat beds farting and burping after they've all eaten and drunk their fine wines. We should put them in economy class rather than have them sleep across the Atlantic.'

'Group travel is just a pain in the bum, unfortunately; when you are selling 96% of seats across the Internet— we do not use travel agents any more—it is very difficult to service it.'

'On the photo identification, we are sorry for the old people who do not have a passport, although it only applies between Ireland and the United Kingdom, but our handling people at Stansted Airport are in an impossible position. We cannot include old age pension books as a form of identification when we are dealing with 16 different countries coming through Stansted. The handling people on the ground simply cannot handle it. It has to be very simple, which is the reason we require a passport, driving licence or the international student card. We do not want the university card or the Blockbuster video card.'

'This bunch of fucking do-gooders in Britain who brought a case against Ryanair, claiming its identification policy discriminates against asylum seekers. What the fuck? These people are in England seeking asylum and now they want to fly around Europe? Well, they can't do it on Ryanair.'

'The Disability Rights Commission wouldn't fucking know how much a wheelchair costs if it jumped up and bit them. We estimate it costs £25 per person to transport disabled passengers, and we carry 1.5 million such passengers every year. Prior to the Bob Ross case we absorbed these costs. We would rather not charge the levy, but we kept getting people who just didn't fancy the long walk to the plane and declared themselves to be in need of assistance. You don't expect to turn up at Bluewater shopping centre on the bus and expect the driver to wheel you round the shops. We shouldn't and nor will we be obliged to sell £10 air fares to people who it will then cost us £18 to get them through a building we don't own.'

On poor sales over a bank holiday weekend: 'There's a lot of people who don't have access to a computer, or who aren't on the internet, on a bank holiday. There is an inertia there among people. It's not that they can't afford to go but that they can't be bothered.'

On a one-hour delay on a flight: 'Three dumb bastards decided they're not going to go to the gate on time. It takes us twice as long to get their bags out of the hold. They should be strung up.'

'Ryanair will never fly the Atlantic route because one cannot get there in a Boeing 737, unless one has a very strong tail wind or passengers who can swim the last hour of the flight.'

On a complaint from the Air Transport Users' Council: 'This is just an attempt by an organisation that doesn't represent anybody to generate some publicity.'

On cancelling free flights for life for a passenger who had won them ten years earlier and denying her €400,000 in compensation, though she was subsequently awarded €67,500 by a judge: 'It blew up one weekend. Our records say she called up on the Friday evening of a bank holiday weekend insisting on two flights to Prestwick and we only had two seats left, and we said, "No, you're not getting it, and you have to call in advance." She claimed she had called two weeks earlier and nobody had gotten back to her. We couldn't prove it, she couldn't prove it. The difficulty with the case was that we inherited it from back in the days when nobody in Ryanair had a sheet of paper. The only evidence that she had anything from us was some video clip from the nine o'clock news saying she had free flights for life. There was no terms, no conditions, nothing. We said, "Fuck off." The first I heard I had bullied her was when I read it in the newspapers in Heathrow. I'm not sure how it's possible to bully someone on the telephone. For the three days of the court case we got the worst publicity any company has ever had in its life, our bookings soared by 30% day by day by day. The more we were in court the bigger the bookings were.

I would regret that we put the girl herself through four days of court, which was no great fun. It distracted us for three or four days and now I'm characterised as hating women and all the rest of it. But four hundred grand is four hundred grand. The lady in question was actually looking for between €400,000 and €500,000 and I would rather take the adverse publicity than pay that amount. I would do it today, I would do it tomorrow and I would do it always. Far too many big companies want to lie down for the fear of bad publicity. If it comes down to the difference between €67,500 compared with €400,000 then you would have to say we are very satisfied.'

On funeral-goers being Ryanair's most profitable passengers: 'They book late because they don't tend to have much notice, and they tend to be price-insensitive because they have to travel.'

'Green protesters are our best passengers. They're always flying off to their demonstrations.'

IN-FLIGHT

'You want luxury? Go somewhere else.'

'On board our flights we don't allow anybody to sleep because we are too busy selling them products.'

'If you want a quiet flight, use another airline. Our flights are noisy, full and we are always trying to sell you something.'

'Don't say it's cheap: that's nasty. The first question 99% of people ask is "What is your cheapest fare to x?" Nobody asks us about the wine list.'

'The fact that our tea and coffee supplier is a Fairtrade brand is a welcome bonus, but the decision was based on lowering costs. We'd change to a non-Fairtrade brand in the morning if it was cheaper.'

'At the moment the ice is free, but if we could find a way of targeting a price on it we would.'

'Nothing's for free on Ryanair flights, we sell everything. Not like these idiots in Austrian Airlines.'

On drinking champagne on Ryanair flights: 'You just have to pay five quid for it.'

'We don't have the widest seats and you're not getting any free food on board, bugger off. But you do get a 30-quid fare.'

'For the rugby match next weekend we are inundated with people who never fly Ryanair except once every two years. We get a surge of complaints the week after the home international against England with fellows writing in: "My good man, I have flown around the world for the last 40 years and I have never been charged for a gin and tonic in my life. I am never flying your appalling, grubby little airline ever again." We write back to him saying: "Dear Sir, you paid £19. If you ever get a £19 air fare on Aer Lingus or British Airways, then I promise you we will give you free flights for life."'

'We go baggage handling at the airport once a month in the summer and I never cease to be amazed by the numbers of people who fly in here on €29 and €39 tickets with golf bags the size of cruise missiles and green fee applications for the K Club, Mount Juliet and all these places where the green fees are €130 to €150. You would be amazed at the number of passengers who fly in on Ryanair at €19 and €29 to stay in the Tara Towers, the Berkeley Court and all the other five-star hotels whose names I cannot remember.'

'At Stansted, we're now taking different types of people. We even got a complaint from someone in Holland Park. No, it wasn't Richard Branson. He said it was the first time in 25 years' flying he'd had to pay for a gin and tonic.'

'Five years ago one of our engineers realised that we spent €2.5 million repairing reclining seats. Large people who use reclining seats tend to break the mechanisms. That was when we had 50 aircraft. A few years later if we had 300 aircraft and I thought, shit, we're going to spend €15–20 million repairing these seats. How could we not repair them? We took the revolutionary step of going to Boeing and asking for non-reclining seats so now one of the features of our planes is that they have non-reclining seats.'

'One of the key glitches we had was security checks, because of those of you who throw the rest of your crap in the seat-back pockets. One of the things that affects the aircraft turnaround is that individually they have to go and inspect every single one of those seat back pockets. How the hell could we stop them having to do that? Well, the cabin crew came up with the legendary idea that we could get rid of the seat-back pockets.'

On in-flight telephones: 'People tend to not want to get into long mobile phone discussions with people sitting around them so I think it will be more people sending texts. Why should I care if it is generating some money?'

On in-flight gambling: 'A lot of people are, frankly, bored on flights. We believe they have a high propensity to get involved in all sorts of games. Finding a cheap flight with Ryanair is a racing certainty and now our passengers will have the chance to enjoy a flutter on Ryanair bingo and instant win with just some of the money they have saved. We might have the pilot calling out the bingo numbers.'

On in-flight movies: 'We expect it to make enormous sums of money. We wouldn't do it otherwise. Entertainment is where the real money will be made in future. Unfortunately, for the moment, we think a porn channel is out on taste grounds. But you never know. The sky is the limit here. The potential is enormous. I think these things will become as common as the in-flight magazine.'

Six months later: 'Whilst the trial period was hampered by the lack of content in non-English languages, the uptake among passengers has been lower than expected. We remain believers in the potential of in-flight entertainment, however. As initially with CDs and the iPod, it may take some time for the travelling public in Europe to catch on to the technology.'

'I make the wrong decision on numerous different things. The most recent was when I launched an in-flight entertainment system about a year ago. It was going to be the future of aviation, everybody flying for free but buying movies on board. I was persuaded against my better judgment to put lottery scratch cards on board as well. I said, 'Forget it, they're for morons.' After about three months, nobody was playing the DVDs because everybody was scratching lottery cards. So we took the DVDs off and made more room for scratch cards. If that's what the public wants . . .'

'We are happy to see families opening up tin-foil packs of sandwiches.'

'No, we shouldn't give you a bloody cup of coffee. We only charge €19 for the ticket.'

'We recognise your right to object. But good luck, somebody else will have your seat.'

BAGGAGE

'Some passengers are carrying baggage which is clearly inappropriate.'

'Baggage is a throwback to the era of ocean liners. I'd stand on my head if I could fly with an airline and avoid standing in a check-in queue. People are happy to carry a bag onto buses so why not onto airlines?'

'We want to get rid of hold baggage. It's one of the biggest costs we have. The average stay of our passengers is less than two days so the overwhelming majority don't need big bags. If people feel they must take a lot of luggage, they can fly with our higher-fare competitors. If they want to fly round Europe with us for £5 or £10, they will have to do it Ryanair's way.'

'Half of our passengers don't check in any luggage. Packing luggage into aircraft takes time. If you are a hand-luggage passenger, you will no longer be cross-subsidising passengers with bags. We are not just streamlining check-in, we are eliminating it.'

'People are overly obsessed with charges. They complain we are charging for check-in, but people who use web check-in and only have carry-on luggage are getting even cheaper fares. We are absolutely upfront about charges and the baggage charges and the check-in charges will rise. We will keep raising them until we can persuade the 40% to 50% of passengers who travel with us for one or two days to bring just one carry-on bag.'

'Paying for baggage is logical, because if we can persuade people to fly with what they can carry, we can carve another chunk off costs and take fares lower still. But yes, it generates publicity, and every time we get publicity, good or bad, bookings spike up.'

'The purpose is not to make money from checked-in luggage—the purpose is to get rid of it altogether. Will it piss off people who are going on a two-week holiday to Ibiza? Yes, it probably will. But we don't fly to those charter holiday destinations anyway.'

'We lose less than half of one bag for every 1,000 passengers carried. To put that in context, British Airways loses 26 bags for every 1,000 passengers carried. For every one bag we lose, British Airways loses 50. For every 70 bags that Air France lose, we lose one. One factor is that these airlines offer connections. In part, however, they are just not as good as us at handling the baggage and personal belongings of passengers. They do not have the same commitment to customer service that shines through Ryanair.'

On passengers observed being weighed at Dublin Airport: 'This has given us food for thought. We routinely conduct a survey of the average weight of passengers. It's because we do free seating. Other airlines can disperse passengers around the aircraft but we can't.'

'I can go away for two weeks with just my overnight bag. Instead of packing a hairdryer, why not buy one when you get there?'

'When I travel I take only 2 or 3 kg. My wife always takes more than 15 kg. I don't know why she needs to pack so much. In fact on our last flight together, I too was a victim of our excess baggage charge.'

On his own carry-on baggage: 'Shirts, more jeans, five pairs of socks and five jocks.'

CUSTOMER SERVICE

'Look, you're not getting a refund so fuck off.'

'If a plane is cancelled, will we put you up in an hotel overnight? Absolutely not. If a plane is delayed, will we give you a voucher for a restaurant? Absolutely not.'

'Are we going to apologise when something goes wrong? No, we're fucking not. Please understand. It does not matter how many times you write to us complaining that we wouldn't put you up in a hotel because there was fog in Stansted. You didn't pay us for it.'

'We're a bit more robust in passenger issues, like saying at Beauvais that we weren't putting passengers up in hotels.'

'No, we don't provide accommodation for people if their flight is cancelled. It's unreasonable of passengers to turn up at the airport and expect to be provided with a free cup of tea. People get an apology and the airport restaurant is open.'

'It's not part of our service to provide accommodation or even a cup of tea in the circumstances of a delay. Some people pay as little as £9 return for their fares, so they cannot really expect such extra benefits. It's unreasonable of passengers to turn up at the airport and expect to be provided with a free cup of tea. Go and buy a cup of tea yourself.'

'You'll never find a Ryanair steward pressing a complimentary glass of champagne in your hand or seat pockets containing the last passenger's wet wipes. True, there is no question of even a drinks voucher if your flight is delayed, but what do you expect for an average fare of £28?'

'One will read much of our appalling passenger service.'

'Are we going to say sorry for our lack of customer service? Absolutely not.'

'Our customers are pretty important. When our customers are wrong then we're not shy about telling them they're wrong. If you show up late for the flight, you're not getting on board the flight.'

'We're not going to fall for any of this old management bullshit or MBA rubbish about clichéd concerns for passengers.'

'Our position is simple. Generally speaking, we won't take any phone calls from customers, because they keep you on the bloody phone all day.'

'Do we occasionally piss people off? Of course we do. But most of the time they're asking for a refund on what everyone knows is a non-refundable ticket.'

'The way I see it is, when you book a ticket in the UCI cinema and cancel it you don't get a refund so why should we offer refunds on "non-refund" flights?'

'If you no-show, you've broken the contract, and you're not getting any money back.'

'We don't care if you don't show up.'

On Kerim Chatty, a man stopped at Sweden's Vasteras Airport from boarding a Ryanair flight to Stansted, thanks to a gun found in his bag: 'Of course he's in our passenger figures. We are not going to give him a refund. We are a no-refund airline.'

'We don't fall over ourselves if you say, "My granny fell ill." What part of "no refund" don't you understand?'

'The airport charges and taxes are non-refundable. We do not pay the money to the State. We have no legal advice on the matter. What we used to do, until two years ago when we fell into line with everyone else, was that we offered a refund of the £5 which was subject to a refund administration charge of £5. In other words one was not getting the refund. In the real world we run a low cost operation. We are not setting up a refunds department. Nobody has yet pointed out that it is illegal. If someone points out that it is illegal we will happily change the procedure to comply with the law. It is the same procedure that is followed by most of the other airlines, not that that is our defence. Our defence is that it is agreed to by every passenger, prior to booking. Everybody understands the meaning of 'all the monies are non-refundable.' This is not dissimilar to what happens with concerts in the Point Depot. People can buy their concert ticket three months in advance, but it is then non-refundable. All of the money paid to Ryanair is non-refundable. If passengers do not like this, they can either buy insurance or choose not to fly with us.

They are free to seek the nearest competitive fare. They understand then.'

'The passenger is under the impression that the total air fare paid to us will be non-refundable. We have received less than one complaint per thousand passengers, and less than 1% of those relate to the non-refundability of the taxes, fees and charges. It does not arise as an issue of concern to our passengers. We are growing at a rate of 40% year on year, and we have no complaints from passengers about not getting €5 or whatever back.'

'Our customer charter is almost like a kickback. We had a couple of years of good PR as we've competed with high-fares airlines like British Airways. Then the "yes buts" started this summer. We want to rebut some of the questions that have been asked. The so-called customer service charter held up by EU airlines isn't worth the paper it's written on. We're committing ourselves to being the number one low-fares airline. The comeback is as meaningless as it is with high-fares airlines.'

'We are the only airline that allows flight changes. This is one of the key issues relating to the non-refundability of our tickets. None of Ryanair's tickets are refundable. The entire price of the ticket is non-refundable, not just the Government or airport taxes. If passengers do not show up, they do not get their money back. A lot of people do not seem to understand that no refund means no refund. However, unlike with every other airline in Europe, up to three hours prior to their departure time, passengers can change the time and date of their flights and change the name on the ticket. So if a passenger's granny has become ill in Mullingar, he or she can call us up to three hours prior to the departure of the flight and change the dates. Passengers can give the ticket to their mammy if they want, and she can then travel in two or three weeks' time.'

'We deliver on-time performance. We tell passengers the precise reasons for any delay through our online flight information system that is updated every five minutes. We can respond to passengers faster than the high-fares airlines, and we have a 100% record of replying within seven days. We provide very prompt refunds. I know somebody will interject that we do not offer refunds, but we do offer refunds in cases where we screw up. If a flight is cancelled because of fog, snow or other weather conditions in a German airport, for example, we will give passengers the option of a refund or a transfer to the nearest available flight. Aside from the death of an immediate relative, those are the only circumstances in which we provide refunds.'

'The quid pro quo for not having refunds is that we do not over-book flights. One of the issues that bedevils most airlines is the over-booking of flights. They know that 6% or 7% of their passengers will not show up, so they over-book the flight by 5% or 6% to ensure that it will be close to 100% full. A lot of business-class fares are fully flexible anyway, and businesspeople will book them and then just not show up or change the flights. We do not do that. We do not allow rich businessmen to change flights. They must buy tickets and change them on the exact same basis as everybody else by calling us three hours in advance. The upside is that people do not get bumped off Ryanair flights because rich businessmen are paying us money. A person paying a fare of €1 has the same entitlements as the rich businessman.'

'We are the only airline to publish our monthly service statistics and we support the EU plan for all airlines to publish them. Funnily enough, none of the high-fare airlines in Europe support this. The Association of European Airlines represents all the high-fares airlines, but Aer Lingus is the only member that does not declare to the association the statistics on its on-time perform-ance. People can read into that what they may. Ryanair's on-time performance in January was 88%. We have been the number one in Europe in this regard for about the last five years. Yet, we are bedevilled with a reputation in this country for always being late. In fact, we are always early in comparison to everybody else.'

'The perception is that Ryanair cancels flights at the drop of a hat because it does not have enough passengers to fill a flight. Ryanair has the highest load factor of any airline in the world. Our year-round load factor is 86%. We do not have flights with no passengers on them. The situation probably never arises in an entire year where we can merge two flights together. Even if it did, we still would not do it. In January, we cancelled less than 0.1% of all the flights scheduled to operate. It was the best performance of any airline in Europe. Unfortunately, Aer Lingus does not release its statistics to their own associ-ation, but Lufthansa cancels about 3% of flights and British Airways also cancels about 3%.'

'Once you give passengers choice and low fares and efficient on-time service—we're beating back customers over here. Our load factors in July and August were at 95%. Statistically, it's almost an impossibility.'

'We have very few complaints. Almost none are about out-of-the-way airports or the kind of apocryphal tales you're always reading.'

'One will read much of our frequently quoted disregard for our customers, yet, statistically, we provide the number one on-time service, we continuously offer the lowest fares and we have the lowest costs. We're in this to make money and provide a service. The more service we provide, the more money we make. We are not perfect, but we do offer a very cheap service and the level of complaints is lower than any other airline, including British Airways.'

On Ryanair finishing last in an airline passenger survey:
'You get some obscure website which claims some 4,000 people participated, when it's more like 400 people, and the reality is that you get more publicity in these kinds of surveys by finishing last than first. The respondents were probably all British Airways employees.'

'We don't "claim" to be the number one on-time airline. The official statistics of the Civil Aviation Authority confirm that Ryanair is the number one on-time airline.'

'The high-fares airlines and the EU got together and came up with a passenger charter. This is the most vacuous document ever agreed between a bunch of airlines and civil servants. It means absolutely nothing. There is nothing in the charter whatsoever. It commits them to very little except to reply to customer complaints and provide refunds within 28 days. We have refused to sign up to this charter because it is meaningless. We have produced our own customer charter, which offers passengers a much more comprehensive package of customer service.'

'Our customer service is about the most well-defined in the world. We guarantee to give you the lowest airfare. You get a safe flight. You normally get an on-time flight. That's the package. We don't and won't give you anything more on top of that. We care for our customers in the most fundamental way possible: we don't screw them every time we fly them.'

'Our customer service is the lowest prices guaranteed, on brand-new aircraft, flying safely, on time, with the least risk of a cancellation or a lost bag. Did you get that service? Yes, you did? Fine. Shut up and go away.'

'You want safe, reliable, on-time, punctual, show up, shut up and get there.'

PILOTS

'People ask how we can have such low fares. I tell them our pilots work for nothing.'

'If this is such a Siberian salt mine and I am such an ogre then why are they still working for the airline? If any of our fellas aren't happy with the current arrangement then they're free to go elsewhere. Godspeed to them. But don't forget that SAS let 150 pilots go in the past six months; Jetmagic in Ireland has gone bust and Flying Finn is close to bankruptcy so there aren't a lot of airlines hiring at the moment.'

'You can't fly any faster or slower even if you wanted to because there is a two-minute separation time between planes going in to land. Our pilots are under less pressure because we don't operate to the busiest airports like Heathrow, Charles de Gaulle or Frankfurt. I don't even know how we would put our pilots under pressure. What do you do? Call him up as he's coming in to land? The only pressure that pilots are under is to prioritise safety.'

'The maximum number of flying hours is 900 a year, divided by 46 weeks: 18 hours a week. People don't understand. There's a reason there's a legal maximum: you can't go over it. It's designed to ensure that they are rested. Pilots are paid €100,000 a year for flying 18 hours a week. How could you be fatigued working nine days in every two weeks?'

'It's quite extraordinary that Ryanair's pilots would fail to accept a five-year pay package which included all captains rising to a salary of £100,000 per annum. They can afford to buy yachts.'

On charging £50 to those who apply for pilot jobs: 'It's to weed out the timewasters. We had 8,500 applications for 60 jobs and got 600 from people under 16 who didn't even have a driving licence. We're trying to get rid of all the loonies, so from now on if you want to apply you have to pay. It's just one of the ways we try to slim down the whole operation and eliminate all the spam.'

On a pilot switching on the Fasten Seatbelts sign to go to the toilet mid-flight: 'Look, even the captain has to take a leak occasionally. When such times arise, it is normal procedure to switch the seatbelt sign on to ensure all passengers are seated. I agree it's not ideal interrupting customers mid-pee for the captain, but it's all part of ensuring a fast turnaround at the other end.'

On a dangerous flying incident at Cork Airport: 'We sent a memo to pilots saying that if you are not properly aligned at 500 feet, you must go around. What we had in these cases was jet jockeys deciding, "I am better than Ryanair standard operating procedures." We don't want anybody doing that. There will be more incidents in the future, no more than British Airways or easyJet. You cannot run any airline the size of ours without someone breaking a rule somewhere.'

On a Ryanair plane landing at the wrong airport: 'The pilot seems to have made a stupid mistake.'

On Aer Lingus pilots: 'Overpaid, underworked peacocks.'

On BALPA, *the British Air Line Pilots Association:* 'The British Airways Low-Pay Association.'

On the creation of a pan-European Ryanair pilots' association: 'Frankly, the response will be "piss off". That's spelt P, asterisk, asterisk, asterisk, off.'

'I don't give a shite if nobody likes me. I am not a cloud bunny, I am not an aerosexual. I don't like aeroplanes. I never wanted to be a pilot like those other platoons of goons who populate the airline industry.'

STAFF

'We are seriously considering making this the new in-flight uniform.'

'At various stages during the year, if I am out there shooting my mouth off, as I have a tendency to do, employees in the pubs are asked, "And where do you work?", and sometimes when they say Ryanair the response is negative. The people who work in Ryanair do not get the recognition in this country that they deserve for the outstanding job they do.'

'I enjoyed hearing that I had a complex about what people think of me. I do not give a hoot what people think of me. I care passionately about what people think about Ryanair in Ireland because we have fantastic people there.'

'People here may have a view about Ryanair and about me—they are free to have whatever view they like about me—but no one can take away the success which the 1,800 people in Ryanair have achieved in recent years. Some would say it is because of me, while many would say it is despite me. We have 1,800 Irish people running the most successful airline in the world.'

'The average pay in Ryanair is now higher than the average pay in Lufthansa, British Airways, Air France and even Aer Lingus, yet we have an image—portrayed mainly by the unions here—of being a low-pay, bucket-shop employer.'

'You can't lead 4,000 people in a direction they don't want to go.'

'We do not have any hard-and-fast rules on employing new staff on the same terms as existing staff. We do not do any union demarcation bullshit here. We have never had a strike in 20 years because we don't have somebody in the middle telling us lies.'

'We are an embarrassment to a lot of trade unions.'

On David Begg, head of the Irish Congress of Trade Unions and a non-executive director of Aer Lingus: 'It is entertaining to listen to Mr Begg lecture the Government, employers and everybody else about "fat cat" pay when his non-executive director's fees at Aer Lingus are one and a half times the average industrial wage, and have risen by 150% in the last 12 months. Mr Begg has his snout firmly buried in the directors' fee trough at Aer Lingus.'

On a SIPTU trade union leader who flies Aer Lingus: 'If Mr Geraghty was not flying on Ryanair, were the hard-earned dues of the union members being frittered away on higher fares for SIPTU bigwigs? Did Mr Geraghty get a special deal on Aer Lingus and travel with the other fat cats in business class?'

On SIPTU: 'It stands for "Stopping Irish People from Travelling".'

On national broadcaster RTÉ: 'Radio Siptu.'

On a strike by baggage handlers at Dublin Airport: 'What the unions got up to in the end was a joke. They closed the airport, CIÉ was dumping all the auld ones down at the roundabout. A couple of our crew got physically assaulted by the head-bangers down there. We are the only airline flying. Eventually Aer Lingus walked off. The whole thing came to a ball of wax. The unions, with Aer Rianta, had ruled Dublin Airport and Aer Lingus for years. We stood out like a sore thumb—an oasis of efficiency with a different way of doing things. It was a public relations disaster. The media refused to see there were 900 employees and 871 of them worked normally. Nobody wanted to represent the side of 871 of our people. If you worked for Ryanair during that period every time you opened a newspaper you would read, "Oh, Ryanair mistreated the workers." At one stage they were saying that we were paying peanuts and getting monkeys to work for us. People would find themselves in pubs and night-clubs at the weekends and all of a sudden they were ashamed to say that they worked for Ryanair. It was a very difficult time. I made the clear mistake that this dispute would run out of steam and go away, and that the only audience we needed to focus on was our employees. I was surprised at how biased the media coverage was.'

'Each of our employees looks after 10,000 passengers per year. In contrast each easyJet employee looks after 6,000 passengers. Each Southwest employee looks after 2,220 passengers. In flag-carriers like Aer Lingus and BA each employee looks after 800 passengers. But we sub-contract work like baggage handling and our standard aircraft size is bigger than our competitors', so our staff don't work that hard.'

'We are the highest-pay airline in Europe and we are also the most productive. This year Ryanair will carry about 10,000 passengers for every employee. The equivalent figure for Aer Lingus, British Airways, Air France and Lufthansa is less than 1,000—one-tenth of our productivity.'

'We employ 1,800 people—you will get your happy people and your cheesed-off ones. But we have got excellent conditions.'

'Highlighters and Post-It Notes are the biggest waste of money ever invented. We use our own biros and I tell the staff not to buy them, just to pick them up from hotels, legal offices, wherever. That's what I do. Recently I did an interview with The Wall Street Journal and I was sitting there with a hotel pen I'd nicked from somewhere. I was asked why and I said: "We at Ryanair have a policy of stealing hotel pens. We won't pay for Bic biros as part of our obsession with low costs."'

On cancelling a staff Christmas party: 'We wanted people to realise that times are tough and this sends the message internally that it's a hard world and we cannot be complacent.'

'A staff pay freeze is a pretty good outcome. If profits were to fall by something like 50% in the next 12 months, it won't be a pay freeze next year, it'll be a pay cut.'

On how to keep employees motivated and happy: 'Fear.'

AIRCRAFT

'We love Boeing. Fuck the French.'

'The thing that made Ryanair stand out from the crowd in Europe, instead of being just another shitty European regional airline, was our decision back in 1994 to go with Boeings 737s.'

'We are an oasis of Boeings in a sea of Airbuses all over Europe. We are an oasis of punctuality and profitability in a sea of losses and shitty delays all over Europe. And I can't fly the bloody things. I can't even turn them on.'

To Boeing workers in Seattle whilst wearing a Ryanair Loves Boeing T-shirt: 'I promise I won't say anything like "Screw Airbus". Bravo Boeing! Adios Airbus! The Irish are with you, not those bastards at Airbus. We have rejected them. They are crap. I will do Riverdance.'

'I don't know if there is anyone here in the Boeing factory who has anything to do with the installation of the forward air stairs—if there is I'd like you to stick your hands up so that I know where you're sitting, cos when

I'm finished talking here, I'm coming after you people.'

'Boeing made a lot of bullshit promises in 1999 but uniquely in the history of aviation they have beaten them. This is the best bloody aircraft in the world for short-haul operations. You people build the best god-damn aircraft in the world. My three favourite words are "Made in Seattle".'

'The message to Boeing today is: "You keep building them, we'll keep buying them" and together, both of us will kick the crap out of Airbus in Europe.'

'Airbus believes Europe is Airbus country. Ryanair believes Europe is Boeing country. Ryanair is going to be working with Boeing on a special mission: kicking the ass of Airbus customers and Airbus all over Europe.'

'The Irish built most of the roads in America and most of the railways in America until the Chinese came along and undercut us and we are confident we will build the biggest scheduled airline in Europe with Boeing's help.'

On collecting a Boeing 737 in Seattle: 'It will be christened DAC, short for "Driving Airbus Crazy".'

'Boeing recognised it needed to have a customer in Europe to help it kick Airbus' ass.'

'Boeing are being eaten alive by Airbus because Airbus know how to do a deal.'

On ordering $9 billion worth of new aircraft from Boeing at half-price: 'One of many natural advantages I have is that I grew up in Mullingar and farmers know that the time to buy is when everyone else is selling and the time to sell is when everyone else is buying. It was quite simple. We had money. Boeing and Airbus couldn't give away planes. So we went and bought up about two years' worth of production. We raped them. I wouldn't even tell my priest what discount I got.'

On announcing a large aircraft order beside David Bonderman, Chairman of Ryanair: 'He's a lot richer than me and we need the guy with the big cheque book to show up for the big ticket items.'

On ordering more aircraft from Boeing: 'The process has started, which I think is better than not talking at all. It's the first round of discussion, so we're making unreasonable demands and Boeing are giving us some reasonable rejections. What we said to Boeing is: "Let's get together towards the end of the year. We could certainly take more planes, but you've got to persuade us."'

'Some fellow added two and two together and got 5225. Are we in discussions with the owners of used aircraft? Yes. Are we in discussions with the owners of new aircraft? Yes. But we won't make any decisions until the price is right and that could be soon or it could be months away.'

'The average hours per year on a Ryanair aircraft is 2,600. I have absolutely no idea how many hours the Irish Government jet runs up. We have offered our services to negotiate with Boeing on the Government's behalf but it has not been taken up yet.'

After 9/11: 'I think we must be the only airline in the world buying aircraft at this moment. In recent months, aircraft prices have crashed. All of a sudden the manufacturers are starting to feel the cold draught. Fortune favours the brave. The time to buy aircraft is when everyone else is selling and prices are low. I believe this is one of those times.'

'We are talking to Boeing about speeding up orders and, in fact, taking in more aircraft. If we are aggressive now in expanding, we are going to make a bloody fortune.'

On divulging that second-hand Ryanair aircraft can be sold for more than the cost of buying new aircraft: 'What I am about to tell you is confidential so please do not repeat this outside this room.'

On offering advice to the chief executive of Air Asia: 'Just fucking buy Boeing.'

'Ryanair will never fly two types of aircraft, but that's not to say we would never switch. It would take a few years to make a smooth changeover, but if it made sense we'd do it without hesitation.'

On the Airbus A320: 'I've heard a lot of horseshit about a wider fuselage. I've yet in 15 years in this industry to meet one passenger who booked his ticket based on that. The seats have been wide enough and the aisles have been wide enough for passengers.'

CHILDHOOD

'I was useless when it came to drinking and girls, but after two years at Trinity I was an expert.'

'Each of the girls at home got their own rooms and us three boys were always in a black hole of Calcutta. Apparently boys didn't need their privacy at all so we roomed together in the slum. The girls all had their rooms and they were all decorated in flowery wallpaper and posters of pop stars. We were always left in one room together to fight it out amongst ourselves.'

'My mother was the stay-at-home mother, six kids, no help. It was a very democratic family—three boys and three girls. Looking back I don't know how anybody did it, except they all did it in those days. But then she was very good. She kept the show on the road. She is an amazing woman. And with six kids they were frequently decorating houses. We'd trash the place.'

'Things were pretty competitive. If you didn't eat quick, you'd starve. And we played a lot of games out of doors. The only way of child-minding us was for my mother to shout, "Out!"'

'We were comfortable. The wealth came more from the fact that we had a very good family life. We never went on foreign holidays or anything like that but I never wanted for anything and certainly not when it came to educating us and there were six children within eight years. By that standard we were very well off and we were very well taken care of.'

'Unlike a lot of businesspeople I don't look back and say there was some black dark secret in my childhood. I had a very happy childhood. I was reared in very affluent circumstances in Mullingar.'

'I certainly wasn't on a plane when I was a kid. We didn't go on holidays much because farmers tended not to go on too many holidays. And also with six kids I don't think the parents wanted to bring us on holidays.'

'I was only seven years old but I don't think of myself as an abused or battered soul, but if I did get a belt at school I certainly got my spelling right next day. I was pretty good at school but without having to try that hard.'

'They wouldn't have let me into the Scouts.'

'I'm not into art, never have been. I've nothing on the left side of the brain, or whatever side of the brain artistic stuff is on.'

'My father was an extraordinary man. We always lived on a farm so he was always like myself—a bit of an amateur farmer. He was far more talented, I think, than I am. My father used to set up businesses that would be very successful for the first few years and then go bust. When he went bust, he would sell the house, and when he made money he would buy another house. The trouble, like with a lot of entrepreneurs, was that once he had set up a business he started to lose interest in it, or lose money, which is even worse.'

'I learned from my parents the value of hard work.'

'I grew up with the overriding ambition to make a lot of money so that I would never be poor.'

'I grew up in a big family and you were competitive with your brothers and sisters. I knew I was always ambitious and that I always wanted to do something, not be some-body but to do things. At the Christian Brothers I wanted to be on the hurling team, at Clongowes I wanted to be on the rugby team. I wasn't, so I probably came out even more ambitious after that.'

'The first time I saw Clongowes, I was about 11 years old. They drove us up and showed us around. All I could see were football pitches, a swimming pool, tennis courts and as far as I was concerned you can drop me here now and leave. I went there more because it had fantastic sporting facilities, not for any great academic achievement.'

'The funny thing about Clongowes school is that it is now a school for the rich and famous—multi-millionaires' sons go to Clongowes. But when we were there, nobody was there. Then Sir Anthony O'Reilly puts his two kids in and comes in his helicopter and lands on the under-13s' rugby pitch.'

'If you stood out for anything in Clongowes, except for rugby, you learned fairly quickly to stop standing out. If you excelled in anything, you got killed. I was tiny on the rugby pitch so I finished up on the upper thirds for rugby, which was for plodders.'

'I was the son of a guy who couldn't describe what he did. All his businesses had gone bust. So we didn't look

at each other and think, "Fuck me, we're the new elite."
We were just a bunch of scuzzy, pimply teenagers.'

'If you were in the top 10% at school you were a swot; if
you were in the bottom 10% you were a moron, and it
was much better to be in the middle. In a fucked-up way,
I was nobody in school. I was common Joe Soap. I'm still
common Joe Soap. I just got lucky a couple of times.'

'I left Clongowes, frankly, with no ambition. I wanted to
go to college because that's where everybody else was
going. I had this notion in my head I wanted to be a
lawyer or a businessman.'

'I chose to go to Trinity College. I just thought Trinity
was cool and UCD was all industrial. I did get a degree. In
drinking, rugby and chasing girls, although I wasn't
much good at that. I learned absolutely squat about business. We fucked off around the centre of Dublin. I did
four years there and got a 2.1 degree. We were released
out of a boarding school after six years and you couldn't
help yourself. It was fantastic. Without a doubt the best
fuck-up years of my life were in Trinity.'

'In the first year in college the business studies students
mixed in with the sociology students. I wasn't shy about
telling the lecturers or the students they were complete
bloody head bangers. Most of the problems of the world
were due to sociologists. I was forming an independent
spirit of enterprise and let's not be sitting there understanding everybody's problems or listening to bloody
social workers creating more problems. We should go out
and work and get on with it.'

WORKING LIFE

'I was very much like Del Boy in Only Fools and Horses.'

'All this Freudian angsty crap of "Where did it all start?" I didn't have a lot of money. I wanted to make money because we had financial problems when I was growing up. I would have murdered, I would have gone through concrete walls, to make money. When I finished college I thought, I'm a fucking genius here, I'll have my pick of these jobs.'

'I left with no job, and scrambled around all summer until I found one. I knew that in a few years I'd be running the world. Then the phone rang. All these fucking lights were flashing, and I couldn't answer it. I'd done four years of a business degree, but I had to get one of the secretaries to tell me how to answer the phone. I knew it all; then, all of a sudden, I had a handle on the fact I knew very little.'

'Accountancy was fucking dull. I did tax, which was actually very fortuitous because in tax you were working

on accounts all the time. I was never out counting wash-
ers or dipping oil tanks at midnight on New Year's Eve. It
was "Here's a set of accounts, how do we get the tax
down?"'

'The accountancy firm SKC had some brilliant partners,
but some of them were wankers, the greatest fucking
gobshites. The tax partner was very good because he
should have thrown me out at that stage. But I would
work long hours and I was very good at racking up the
time, which in accountancy firms means money.'

'In those days there were only two ways of making
money—retail or drink. I didn't have the money to buy
a pub so I bought a newsagent. You could buy up an old
newsagent and do them up, extend the opening hours
and bang up the turnover. I bought mom-and-pop out-
fits; open at seven in the morning, close at 11 at night, treble the turnover, treble your money.'

'The first person I ever looked up to in my business
life was the bank manager of Allied Irish Bank in
Walkinstown, who gave me a £25,000 overdraft to buy
the shop. Boy did I look up to him. My ass was grass if
I didn't pay back that 25-grand overdraft in 18 months.'

'I was going around in this van that had no back seat in
it, going up and down to Musgrave's getting all the cash
and carry stuff. It wasn't very glorious.'

'Being a greedy little bugger like I was at the time, we
decided to open on Christmas Day. By lunchtime on
Christmas Day we had been cleaned out of chocolates,
batteries and cigarettes. We took £14,000 in that day, 14
times the normal day's turnover.'

'I never had a sexual experience in my life like that. The
feeling of having one wad of notes pushed down one side

of my trousers and another wad of notes down the other, waddling out of the newsagents in Walkinstown with 14 grand, hoping I wasn't going to be mugged going to the car.'

'I was bored but it was very good money. I just wanted to make a lot of money by the time I was 30.'

EARLY RYANAIR

'The only thing I will not do is fly the aircraft.'

'I started to work for Tony Ryan in 1987 and that is how I got into aviation. Tony Ryan is a genius. I learnt an awful lot from him. You get few opportunities in life to learn from someone so rich and successful. I get on with him half the time and I fight with him the other half.'

On Tony Ryan: 'I was brought along as the gofer. I was very impressed by him because he was rich, successful and was running a company that had terrific mystique. Nobody knew what the hell aircraft leasing was. He was the first businessman I'd met who had this global ambition. Everybody else was worried about the cost of women's knickers and the cost of this, that and the other. He had maps of the world looking at where he could lease aircraft. It was revolutionary in the mid-1980s because Ireland back then was very insular. He was one of only a few businessmen putting an Irish stamp on the world. I was begging him, "Shut the airline down, close it down, it will never make money." It was doomed. Tony was the only person who said no, partly because his name was on the side of it but also partly, I think, because he didn't like being beaten. He wasn't going to be beaten by the Government and the State monopoly. He had great balls.'

'I couldn't get a real job. It just sort of fell out of the sky. My title was bagman. I was based on the farm in Tipperary—the job was anything from hunting cattle, running errands, doing tax returns.'

'They lost the run of themselves. Tony has never been a great man to focus on cost. He wanted it to be elegant, to deliver a better service, business class and frequent flyer club; I mean complete bloody nonsense, to serve nice china mugs and slippers but charge 10 quid. You can decide to either be Marks & Spencer or be Fortnum & Mason but you can't be something in between.'

'When I first arrived at Ryanair it was like you'd arrived at the pearly gates. There was a gorgeous blonde chick at every desk. The place was a shambles yet it was still amazingly sexy.'

'Ryanair was set up originally to take on Aer Lingus and British Airways on the Dublin to London route and offer low fares but they kind of lost the plot a bit. They were opening routes fucking left, right and centre, the route network was nuts. They had no fucking schedule at all. It was madness. It was all planes, planes, planes and no airline.'

'We were trying to do what many other airlines were trying to do in Europe, which was to be a slightly lower-fare "me too" carrier to Aer Lingus or British Airways. But the fares were about 20% cheaper, which meant we just lost more money than they did.'

'The place was in a mess. There was no cost control. They were trying to be a me-too airline like everyone else and not really succeeding very well with it.'

'The accounts were rubbish. There was nobody collecting cash. We didn't know how much money we had, except that we had nothing in the bank. The bottom line was that if Tony Ryan didn't give us a million quid by next Friday we couldn't pay the wages.'

'There was a hole in this fucking company. Where the fuck was our money?'

'We actually came to a point one night where we bounced a cheque to Aer Rianta for £24,000. They said if the cheque didn't go through on Friday they were going to put a yoke on the front of the plane and seize it.'

'It was all about getting rid of the lunatics who were running the asylum and putting some order on it. I was doing a lot of ripping and burning and slashing.'

'I kept trying to get out. I thought it was a stupid business, and also it was very high-profile. I didn't want a high profile; I wanted to make lots of money but not be known. That was the way my family would operate; there was no credit for being in the newspapers.'

'My role in Ryanair from 1988 to 1991 was to stop it losing money—it wasn't looking to make Tony Ryan money. We were hovering on the verge of bankruptcy. In Spring 1991 I thought it would be a miracle if we were still in business three months later.'

'I thought that if I got it right I could make some decent money, but not a fortune. I thought in a good year we'd make a couple of million and I'd get £250,000, and there you go, more money than I could imagine, I'd be rich. But at that stage it was as likely to go bust as it was to make a million quid.'

'There wasn't any great foresight on my part. Over two or three years three of us together did turn the airline around and put it on the footing it is on today. I get far too much credit for being the turnaround artist.'

'Looking back it looks like we were some kind of genius turnaround artists whereas in fact the company was in such a sorry state that all we did was try to keep improving it day by day.'

'I was trying to get out. I wanted out all the time. I had four years of this place on the brink of bankruptcy. We had gotten it back to making a small profit, and I had had enough.'

'Close it down, because you couldn't give it away. I thought it was beyond rescue.'

'I didn't particularly want a job in the company that I was recommending should be closed down.'

'I said, "Close the fucking airline because it's a basket case." Eventually we made a £10-million profit and the Ryans had to write me a cheque for £3.5 million at which point they said "Hang on."'

'Ryanair will never make money. It will always lose money. It's an airline. Forget it.'

'I joined as a toilet cleaner and I'm still shovelling shit.'

PRESENT RYANAIR

'Everything is profitable for us.'

'Ten years ago the only objective was to survive, to pay next year's bills. Five years ago we just wanted to be bigger than Aer Lingus, and we achieved that. The target in the next five years is to make us the largest scheduled international airline in Europe. We have long since given up wanting to be Ireland's or the UK's biggest airline.'

'Our strategy is about running the airline the way people want. Low fares, high capacity at busy times, flexible tickets. There are only three layers of management. No secrets. No dogma. No unions. I drive buses at the airport, check in passengers, load bags and get a good kicking when I play for the baggage handlers' football team.'

'We can fly six aircraft a day where Aer Lingus or British Airways could fly four. Where they can get six in the air, we fly eight. So we're 20–25% more efficient from the very start. It's so simple a four-year-old could work it out.'

'Some airlines enter a new route and aim to make a profit in three years. We will not enter a route if we cannot break even in three hours and grow the market by at least 100%.'

'We are probably certifiably insane for investing so much money, growing so rapidly, opening up new routes and offering lower fares at a time when there is a world recession, a crisis in Iraq and a feeling of doom and gloom all over the place.'

'We are growing like gangbusters. There is an almost insatiable demand for low-fare air travel.'

'This is not helter-skelter, uncontrollable growth—it is very controlled.'

'There is no cap on us growing at 25% a year for the foreseeable future.'

'Ryanair is going to be a monster in Europe in the next 10 to 12 years.'

'We are up to our goolies at the moment in work.'

'I'm not sure whether we will continue to grow after that by 20% a year if we have reached 70 million passengers. Perhaps it will be only 10% to 15%.'

'Being successful is about having the lowest costs; that means beating the crap out of suppliers, and most of our suppliers are Government-owned airports or agencies, which means we fight constantly with Governments and idiot Brussels bureaucrats who want to put up the cost of travel, or half-witted environmentalists who can't add two and two.'

'I'm not sure what to do after we become the biggest airline in Europe. It will get a bit boring growing at 5%. Other than convincing you guys over our customer service, there will be no more mountains to climb.'

'We go where the costs are lowest and where we can maximise the profit, and I make no apology for that. We will fight anybody, anytime, anywhere about costs. We're in a commodity business now where the lowest cost wins.'

'Some of the urban legends about our famous cost-cutting attitude aren't actually true but we own up to them anyway because they make very good stories. A story circulated in the UK that, as part of our cost-cutting, we were banning people from charging their mobile phones in the office, saving ourselves 0.00002c per day. The PR people wrote up a denial but I said, "Why?" They replied, "Because it makes us look nasty, petty, and cheap." Instead, I issued a press release saying that, absolutely, we ban mobile-phone charging. The more we can sound nasty, petty and cheap, the more we can reinforce in people's minds that we are extremely bloody cheap and they will choose to fly with us.'

'Our success inevitably brings about a time when we're no longer Robin Hood of Sherwood and everybody loves us. We're getting bigger and you have to learn to take the rough with the smooth.'

'We're going to see the bloodbath to end all bloodbaths. The principal cause of the bloodbath is Ryanair. We are going to show up in your market and trash your yields. Yields are soft, the market is soft. We have responded in the only way we know how—by starting a fares war.'

'In many ways we would welcome a chill or something even colder. A recession is now likely; I don't think it can be averted by reducing interest rates. We can't keep bailing ourselves out with these artificial interest-rate cuts. The whole system got very frothy. We would welcome a good, deep recession for 12-18 months. During recessions, travel does not get cut back, but people look for cheaper alternatives. If we get a recession I don't see people cutting back on the amount of flying they do. A little bit of recession would be very good for the economy.'

'I love this. It is much more fun when the world is falling apart than when things are boring and going well. We had been saying fares and margins would fall. What we didn't foresee was that they would come down this bloody quickly.'

'For the first three or four years of the Internet I blocked any internet development here. When easyJet first started off with its site, I said we are not doing the internet for a very sane and obvious reason. At that stage 60% of our sales were driven through travel agents. The software didn't exist to sell half your tickets online. If you were selling through the travel agents you had to have the old tickets with the dye on the back of them and all our tickets had to be like that. So I said that until we have the technology to get rid of the old tickets, we wait. Then later the technology came along and that's when we went into the internet. It was the right thing to do. We intend to make Ryanair.com the largest air travel website in Europe.'

On the late Dr Tony Ryan: 'I met him last week for a couple of hours in Lyons. Despite the fact that he knew he was dying, he wanted to discuss the strategy for Ryanair, not for next year, but for five and 10 years. He thought we're not growing fast enough and he thought we shouldn't confine ourselves to Europe. He still thought I wasn't doing a good job. As with everything else, he thought that we should be doing it better, improving customer service, lowering prices and trying to revolutionise the industry again in the next 10 years in much the same way as he has lead the revolution in the last 10.'

On the biggest risk to Ryanair's expansion: 'Me. Management indiscipline. If we get sloppy, start winning awards, pontificating, writing books, building new headquarters, dating pop stars—sorry, that's OK—then I think we're dead. Or the danger is that we screw this up ourselves, like the chief executive writes a book on how to run airlines. Then we're really screwed.'

'The big objective now is "don't screw it up". Hopefully, we won't start to believe our own bullshit.'

'Safety is the number one issue. The other thing is if management gets fat, lazy and sloppy and starts doing things like joining the IMI.'

'I will be worried if we get fat and lazy and start playing golf and giving lots of conference speeches and move into palatial new headquarters.'

On his vision for Ryanair: 'World domination. Europe, then the world and then the universe.'

On being asked what catastrophic event could destroy Ryanair: 'I suppose we could join IBEC.'

On how Ryanair might fail: 'Nuclear war in Europe, an accident by ourselves or some other low-fares carrier in Europe or believing our own bullshit.'

'My role in making Ryanair succeed is to interfere as little as possible, try to stay out of other people's way and then claim the credit for all the success when it comes along.'

INVESTORS

'There is a lot of bullshit out there and, to be honest, I don't know where it is coming from.'

'I am delighted to say we are number one for profitability and market capitalisation. The word 'profitability' is often portrayed as a dirty word here but I fail to see why one is in business if one is not in business to make money.'

On beginning a press conference to announce results: 'I'm here with Howard Millar and Michael Cawley, our two deputy chief executives. But they're presently making love in the gentlemen's toilets, such is their excitement at today's results.'

'People look at 20% profit margins in the airline business and they assume you are smuggling drugs or doing something naughty with the figures.'

'Any idiot can paint a plane and start out offering low fares. It's about sustainability. We've been profitable now for 20 years.'

'We expect our profits to grow by 20–25%. That's not just good, that's practically obscene in an industry in which few people make money. This isn't an airline, it's a drug baron's business.'

'We could not sell tickets for a year and still have cash in the bank.'

'These are very good numbers; the model is very strong; nobody comes remotely close to us in Europe; but can everybody please keep their feet on the ground. We have a very highly rated share at the moment, but at the end of the day we want everyone to remember it's an airline and not some kind of tech stock.'

'If you look at the US, there are around 850 Boeing 737 and Airbus comparators in use by low-cost carriers. In Europe it is 320, and the population here is larger. That does not mean that everyone is going to grow at the same time. Ryanair and easyJet are taking about 25 planes each a year for the next few years. Overall there is scope for tremendous growth.'

'Gradually we will expand across Europe, as we already are aggressively now. And because our unit prices and unit costs are so much lower, nobody else can compete with us. There's only Ryanair when it comes to low fares.'

'I've said it before, and I'll say it again; I don't see any requirement for us doing a rights issue. At current price levels, if we were to issue even one new share for every one currently in issue, we would raise over £900 million, and we wouldn't know what to do with that amount of capital.'

'Our stock price jumped up. I think we closed today at €8.80. It takes analysts a while to digest things. If they had a good understanding of the business they would not be analysts.'

On his company accounts: 'It's perfectly straightforward. Ebitda? That's some bloody number I don't understand.'

At a press conference to float Ryanair: 'You're probably wondering why we're suddenly talking to everybody for the first time in 10 years. When this is finished we'll probably disappear for another 10 years.'

'I am ashamed to say I do not know the current market capitalisation of Ryanair. The last time I looked it was about €4 billion but it is going up and down frequently given the situation in Iraq.'

'We are never paying a dividend as long as I live and breathe and as long as I'm the largest individual shareholder. If you are stupid enough to invest in an airline for its dividend flow you should be put back in the loony bin where you came from. There's no reliable stream for a dividend.'

On a Ryanair profits warning: 'Hey, live with it. Remember Tesco had a drop in profits four years ago and nobody said its business model was bust. It is our job to show that this is a bump in the road and not some hole we have fallen into. We are still going to make 10% profit margins after tax. No other airline in the world makes that, so is our business model bust? No, it isn't.'

'Everyone has a blip. There is a price war out there that we are causing, leading and winning.'

'Screw the share price. We're in a fares war. I own more of the shares than anyone else. They can join the queue behind me. We are in a fares war and we are going to win it. If they are not happy, they can always sell their shares.'

'The next 12 months will not be pretty for net profit and will not be pretty for shareholders.'

'If we lose money in the fourth quarter, the rest of the world will be blowing its brains out.'

'It's like Southwest in the US. When they first went into California, their stock price fell by 40% to 50% due to fare wars with the likes of the United Airlines shuttle and other California carriers. Ten years later, Southwest owned California. Any share price jumps up and down, and ours is no exception. But as long as the basic business model is sound and you're executing it properly, nothing will stop you.'

'There's no harm making a quarterly loss once in a while. The time you test the mettle of a company is when it's losing money.'

'There is absolutely no harm in losing the mythical horseshit that we can walk on water. Given that this is our first profits warning, the market went nuts. But there is no point whingeing that everybody has got it in for us. Perhaps we deserved a slap around the head. It was inevitable that at some point in our history, profits would stop accelerating.'

'There are commentators and analysts who think we've had a very good run for a long time and it's all really a house of cards and there's something funny and it can't last. There are lots of people waiting for us to blow up.'

'Any chief executive who doesn't have a sense of their own mortality is heading for disaster. They read articles describing themselves as visionaries and geniuses. They shouldn't believe it any more than when the press are calling them gobshites and wankers.'

CORPORATE LIFE

*'This will be my
first and last
speech.'*

'**B**usiness is simple. You buy it for this, you sell it for that,
and the bit in the middle is ultimately your profit or
loss. We have low-cost aircraft, low-cost airport deals, we
don't provide frills, we pay travel agents less, our people are
well paid but work hard and we deal in efficiencies. A second low-cost airline will only survive in Ireland as long as
it is prepared to keep losing money. Britain is a tougher
market, but even there nobody can match our efficiency.'

'The meek may inherit the earth, but they will not have
it for long.'

'We try to keep a lot of the bull out of the organisation.
We keep the management structure extremely flat. As we
grow, we're only adding aircraft, pilots, in-flight people
and engineers. We don't need these layers of bureaucracy
or layers of management.'

'Hopefully we avoid the bull by keeping our feet on the ground and not losing the run of ourselves. The downside of success that we really worry about is the danger that the more successful you are, the more likely you are to lose sight of the things that made you successful.'

'Having a long term plan is a waste of time. I'm not a thinker. You see opportunities and you try to take them. There's no point having some long-term plan because a long-term plan gets knocked on its ass.'

'You won't get anywhere settling for mediocrity or simply getting by.'

On decision-making: 'Recognise you are wrong, and stop doing whatever it is that is wrong.'

'There's an awful lot of bullshit talked about brands. Ryanair is a pretty good, anodyne brand that works across Europe. We have no intention of changing the brand or redesigning the image or the rest of that old nonsense. In my 13 years at this company, Aer Lingus has changed its branding three times, British Airways has changed three times, we've not changed it once, and the virtue of what we've done has been proven. People don't fly with Ryanair because of our image or our brand, they fly because we guarantee them the lowest fares; when you get on the aircraft it's clean, it's bright, it's safe and it's reliable.'

On corporate governance: 'Those are the kinds of questions you ask companies that are about to go bankrupt, not one that is making more than €200 million a year in profit and has €1.1 billion in cash on its balance sheet.'

On Enron: 'At Ryanair, everything is on the balance sheet. We are from the country that in recent weeks gave you Elan and AIB. Ryanair has not succumbed to Enronitis.

For the ninth year on the trot our net margin actual profits after tax is 21% and that does not go into my pocket, where I think it belongs, but onto the balance sheet.'

On advertising agencies: 'They were all the same. They were 40-year-old men with ponytails, black suits, black T-shirts and a big buckle on their belt.'

On consultants: 'The worst are change-management consultants. What is that? I believe hiring consultants is an abdication by management of their responsibilities. If the consultant is so good at managing change, then why not hire him to run the company and do it himself? The airline industry worldwide has lost more money since 1985 than its entire accumulated profits since the flight of Alcock and Brown. Every idiot who gets fired in the industry shows up as a consultant somewhere. I would shoot any consultant who came through my door.'

'Business books are bullshit and are usually written by wankers.'

On not using email: 'My inbox just fills up with shite.'

On winning the European Business Campaigner of the Year award: 'Business Campaigner? More like Business Complainer of the Year.'

On winning the Sunday Telegraph Business Leader of the Year Award: 'I am deeply humbled, but surely we are doomed. It is the kiss of death, it must be all downhill from now since we have won an award. An element of that is true. There are three signs you need to be wary of when looking at a business—when it buys a company helicopter, moves into plush new headquarters and when it wins awards. It usually tends to lead to complacency in the company or from the gobshite who wins it. But I was a gobshite anyway.'

OIL

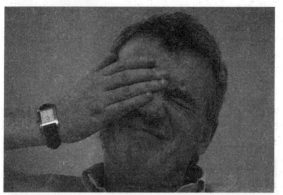

'Jesus, we don't look bright.'

'If we were bright, we wouldn't be working for airlines. We're no experts on oil prices here. Frankly, we'll never get it right. It's an inability to hedge properly. We would have done better if we had waited another week. We could be hedging today at $68 a barrel. As every dollar is about €3 million, we could have saved ourselves €15 million. If it keeps falling we have done a bad job. If anyone shoots someone and the price goes back up then we've done a good job.'

'Fuel has improved a little bit. But it is fluctuating around so wildly there is no point in worrying about it.'

'If oil goes to $75 a barrel we'll still be the only break-even airline in Europe, but at that stage we'll probably be the only airline in Europe still flying. We would welcome higher fuel charges. It would put some of the flaky operators out of business.'

'Ryanair has the biggest profit margins among airlines, of 20% after tax. So, we can absorb higher oil prices much more easily. Most other airlines have margins of 4% or 5%.'

'The key to Ryanair's traffic and profit growth was our refusal to levy fuel surcharges on our passengers at a time when most other airlines in Europe are introducing or increasing them. In some cases, other airlines' surcharges exceed our average fares.'

'High oil prices are good for us and they are bad for competitors. It doesn't affect us. We are fully hedged. We are delighted with the rise. It's great as it will knock the crap out of most rival airlines. It will hasten the demise of the basket cases. The sooner they go to the wall the better.'

'The price of oil is likely to go higher throughout the winter. I would be surprised if the traders don't manage to put it past the $100 barrier at some point. It doesn't affect us at Ryanair. We are fully hedged until next March. We are delighted with the rise. Everybody thought Goldman Sachs were mad when they predicted $100 a barrel in the spring. Now they do not look so stupid.'

'I've now come to the view that I hope oil does stay at $125 or $130 a barrel because I think that will bankrupt half of the airlines flying today. In which case we'll still be the lowest-fares airline in Europe, but our fares won't be €40 a passenger. They might be a little bit higher.'

'With oil at $125 a barrel we certainly won't make a lot of money; I don't think we will lose money. Oil is really hurting us now. I have been wrong about oil for the last 12 months.'

'I reckon we will take our chances on the current price of oil for the rest of the year.'

On whether the price of oil will reach $200 a barrel: 'Anything is possible.'

THE ENVIRONMENT

'I say keep flying.'

'It's July, the press have nothing to write about. The Prime Minister's on holiday, the World Cup is over, Zidane has retired—I know, let's write about the impact of aviation on the environment.'

'The newspapers target airlines as the cause of everything that's bad: pollution, greenhouse gases, emissions, floods, war, pestilence and famine in Darfur.'

'The BBC runs Green Week, ITV runs Greener Week, Sky runs Even Greener Week, Channel 4 runs Even Bloody Greener Week and each time they use a picture of aeroplanes taking off.'

On Sir Nicolas Stern's climate change report: 'There's a lot of misinformation and lies being put about by the eco-nuts in this country on the back of a report put about by an idiot economist. If you listen to them you would think aviation was responsible for melting the polar ice caps, heating up the globe by 2% a year and for every war, pestilence and SARS epidemic.'

'I don't think the advice of a bunch of UN scientists should be taken as gospel truth.'

'There is a fundamental misunderstanding about aviation and environmental taxes at the moment. No one knows what they are talking about.'

'There's a lot of bullshit being peddled, mainly by environmental nutters, that aviation is the cause of global warming, climate change and everything else.'

'Remember all these green protestors still take flights to go on their eco-tours, and how do you think they get to their demonstrations?'

'The Sustainable Aviation Group, God help us, is another bunch of lemmings shuffling towards a cliff edge. A lot of members of the Sustainable Aviation Group won't be around in 10 years' time. That'll be their main contribution to sustainable aviation.'

'I don't believe in trotting out all that politically correct claptrap just so as not to upset a couple of fucking environmental lunatics. They are just loons.'

'We want to annoy the fuckers whenever we can. The best thing we can do with environmentalists is shoot them. These headbangers want to make air travel the preserve of the rich. They are Luddites marching us back to the 18th century.'

'I listen to all this drivel about turning down the central heating, going back to candles, returning to the dark ages. You do that if you want to. But none of it will make any difference. It just panders to your middle-class, middle-aged angst and guilt.'

'It's crazy that these people in leafy suburbia in the UK think they can fix all the problems.'

'The chattering bloody classes, or what I call the liberal Guardian readers, they're all buying SUVs to drive around the streets of London. And there's this huge disconnect between their stated passion or care for the environment and what they actually do. I smile at these environmental loons who drive their SUVs down to Sainsbury's on a Saturday morning and buy kiwi fruit from New Zealand and kumquats from Latin America. They're flown in from New Zealand for Christ's sake. They're the equivalent of, you know, environmental nuclear bombs! But nobody says, "Let's ban the kiwi fruits."'

'If you're concerned about the environment, stop driving.'

'These hairy environmentalists go to the health store to buy their organic strawberries flown in from South Africa. Why aren't they whacking a huge tax on bananas and grapes from half-way round the world? Why don't they eat British turnips all winter if they want to save air flights? Because they can't live without their scallops from Chile.'

'The Swampies of this world are climbing up trees to protest about airlines and airports. They should all get a job and get a fucking life.'

'I like environmentalists who tell the truth. I dislike and disabuse environmentalists who lie. There is an awful lot of lying going on in the environmental movement.'

'The eco-nutbags blame us for melting the icecaps, war, pestilence and the SARS epidemic when, in reality, the factual information from the EU Environment Agency is that aviation accounts for 2% of greenhouse gas emissions and of CO_2 emissions in the EU. If everybody stopped flying for the next 12 months and CO_2 levels fell by 2%, it would represent less than the oil- and coal-fired stations to be opened by the Chinese in the next 12 months.'

'Coal-fired and oil-fired power stations are the biggest contributor of carbon but I have yet to hear any fearless eco-warriors advocating nuclear power as they drive around in their suvs to their next protest meeting.'

'China and India are laughing at us while they build more coal-fired power stations. The European middle classes are having a mid-life crisis and the sooner we wake up and say so the better. Soon it won't matter how many lights we turn off or how many bicycles we ride or flights we make, the damage will have been done on the other side of the world by a billion people who have only just discovered the delights of turning on lights.'

'CND nutters in the 1970s banged on about being against nuclear war, well, we all were. But the point is you can't change the world by putting on a pair of dungarees or sandals. You need to look at the real culprits and begin negotiations with them.'

'Human breathing is one of the biggest problems, as far as I can see, so why don't the environmentalists just shoot all the humans?'

'Let's go nuclear if you really want to do something and then let's watch the eco-nuts go crazy.'

'I did not suggest that we shoot cows, I simply offered the factual information that since they generated greater emissions than global aviation, perhaps some of these eco-warriors would expect us to shoot all farm animals in pursuit of their misguided, inaccurate and misinformed agenda.'

'Emissions is a load of bollocks talked up by all these sandal-wearing Greens and other headbangers, most of whom fly on Ryanair when they go to protest at G8 meetings. Emissions is just talked about by loonies. It's a lot of hot air. It's the usual horseshit that we hear.'

'I don't think emissions credit trading will come in and anyway I am far too busy doubling Ryanair over the next few years to be joining any carbon emissions trading scheme. It would bankrupt British Airways, Lufthansa and Alitalia. It's lots of political talk. How are you going to get the Italians to pay €22 per tonne, when none of the African or Russian airlines are doing it? Is it going to affect the business? I don't think so. It won't affect the fare differential between Ryanair and British Airways. We'll still grow great guns.'

'We will double our emissions in the next five years because we are doubling our traffic. But if preserving the environment means stopping poor people flying so only the rich can fly, then screw it. People are enjoying low-cost air travel and it creates jobs and tourism, which allows environmentalists to keep their highly paid jobs so they can spend their spare time whingeing about the environment.'

On being branded the 'unacceptable face of capitalism': 'It's a title I won proudly.'

On the UK Government Environment Minister, Ian Pearson: 'He is foolish and ill-informed and hasn't a clue what he's talking about. He talks a lot but does little. Mr Pearson is a Minister of a Government which has, like Scrooge, this Christmas doubled the air passenger tax on tickets from £5 to £10, grabbing another £1 billion in taxes without doing anything whatsoever to invest this money in the environment. It is time Minister Pearson and other equally foolish politicians actually tackled the real cause of climate change, which is road transport and power generation. Being attacked by Mr Pearson is like being savaged by a dead sheep. Mr Pearson was probably interviewed by *The Guardian* late at night in a pub. This is the silly season and you should always start it being abused by some idiot politician somewhere.'

On Ciarán Cuffe TD, *Green Party:* 'I accept that "Green Party—Transport Spokesperson" is an oxymoron. I have no doubt that the people of this island, and particularly our tourism industry, will be rolling around our dole offices laughing at Ciarán Cuffe's vision for "slow travel" by boat and train. Only someone who is hopelessly out of touch with everyday reality, such as Mr Cuffe, who enjoys 22 weeks' holidays a year from the Dáil compared with the ordinary citizen, who has 20 days holidays, could possibly recommend spending 36 hours and over €300 to get to Brussels and another 36 hours back. "Slow travel" would quickly be replaced by "no travel" and no visitors. Now there's a thought for the Greens' transport spokesman to ponder during his next slow train to nowhere.'

'I've heard that Bertie Ahern is now going to go green, which is rich for a Prime Minister who, as recently as three months ago, said he opposed nuclear power. If Bertie really wants to go green, then the biggest polluter in this country is the ESB, which is still running coal- and peat-fired power stations. So if Bertie Ahern really wants to stop talking the talk and maybe walk the walk, let's go and have nuclear power stations here in Ireland. I don't care who builds the power stations because otherwise we, in the next number of years, will be importing power from the UK.'

'It's just politicians pandering to the latest fashion. Gordon Brown wants us all to believe that he spends his days mulching his compost with his children. David Cameron's gone Dutch with his windmills and clogs. Neither of them really means it. They know that changing a lightbulb isn't going to make any difference but a picture of them changing a lightbulb will be a nice, cosy image. The Chancellor is probably the biggest polluter in the UK, given that the Government is responsible for most of the power stations in the country.'

'I don't think it makes any difference who is Prime Minister. Our only difficulty with Gordon Brown is his doubling of the air passenger duty tax. If you want to deal with environmental measures, by all means do, but tax the rich, not the ordinary people. We will be calling for the abolition of the air passenger duty all together. This is just another tax on tourists.'

'All the bloody tree-planting in the world isn't going to make up for our emissions. We have to think of bigger ideas. Mr Brown's proposals won't stop people flying, petrol tax doesn't stop us driving. They are all stealth taxes. The Chancellor is just lying when he says these new taxes are environmental. Mr Brown is not even a light shade of khaki.'

'All this environmental bullshit that has allowed Gordon Brown to double air passenger duty. Gordon Brown has lied. It's just a bloody tax grab. We need a recession if we are going to see off some of this environmental nonsense.'

On the Bishop of London, who said it was sinful to pollute the planet by jetting away on holiday: 'The Bishop of London has got empty churches. Presumably, if no one went on holiday perhaps they might turn up and listen to his sermons. God bless the bishop. The bishops have got their own crosses to bear. Goodness knows what he would know about greenhouse gases. He was obviously at some dinner party with the chatterati. It's the usual clichéd horseshit that we hear.'

'To suggest that I and Ryanair do not have regard for the environment is clearly untrue and damaging to Ryanair's good name and reputation.'

'Aircraft account for a Mickey Mouse 2% of emissions in Europe, motor cars account for 18%. Our planes use a lot less fuel per mile than a one-person car.'

'Over the past five years, Ryanair has achieved a 50% reduction in carbon dioxide emissions and a 45% reduction in fuel burn and noise by investing over $10 billion in brand-new aircraft. Ryanair now operates the youngest, quietest, most fuel-efficient fleet in the industry.'

'It's about time some of the media organisations here addressed this with some factual information instead of just rehashing the mindless and stupid lies being put about by these environmentalists and idiot politicians. We are the greenest and cleanest airline in Europe, and we're putting five million free airline seats on the website today to celebrate that.'

'We carry far more passengers per unit of fuel consumed than cars or buses, which create far more pollution at ground level than we do at 36,000 feet.'

'The skies are empty.'

'There is no relationship between the aviation industry and climate change and global warming.'

'There is no suggestion the eco-loonies are dissuading people from travel.'

'We will have to become more sensitive to all those environmental whingers.'

'If you really want to do something, you could penalise business-class people flying around in low-density seating. If you want to tax anybody, tax the rich, tax business class.'

'Why don't I support anything that increases the cost of flying? Because I run an airline. All I want to do is restore some balance to the debate that the airlines are not the problem. In China, they are opening two coal-fired power stations a week. America hasn't signed up to the Kyoto protocol. Why are we all rolling around pulling wool out of our navels about cheap flights in the UK?'

'Environmentalists are often very aggressive with their baloney, but these numb-nuts don't realise that aviation is already the most taxed form of travel.'

'Aircraft emissions are less than marine transport, and yet I don't see anyone saying, you know, "Let's tax the fuck out of the ferries."'

'Trains are incredibly over-subsidised and don't service people's needs. The trains were fine in Victorian times when if you didn't have a stable you walked, but no one needs to use them now.'

'The people who are worried about the environment are right to be worried. But the self-abusers who think taxing air transport is going to do anything for the environment are eco-nuts.'

'I don't know why we are trying to avert a recession. We need a recession. I think it would be great for the aviation industry. A recession will get rid of environmental taxes and a lot of the environmental nonsense that's talked about regarding aviation.'

'Taxing aviation will not affect the growth of Ryanair one iota. We will continue to grow like gangbusters because the price differential between Ryanair and easyJet and British Airways will not change. If people are serious about tackling the minuscule contribution of aviation, what they ought to be tackling are the operators of the old gas-guzzling aircraft like BA or those who run two flights to get you to your destination, unlike low-fares airlines.'

'We will go from 40 to 80 million passengers in the next few years. We will take them off British Airways and the other old carriers who are flying gas-guzzling, ancient aircraft and pack them into fuel-efficient planes. So Ryanair will be saving the environment—not that we care much.'

SECURITY

'We shall fight them on the beaches, we shall fight them in the air, we shall fight them with toiletries.'

'Generally, the best time to visit anywhere is after a terrorist attack because the hotels are discounting like mad and the place is crawling with security.'

On 9/11: 'There is little doubt that tragic events in the US are being used by a number of European flag-carriers as an excuse upon which to blame their long-standing problems and as an opportunity to look for subsidies and handouts. You could fill every seat but instead there's this attitude that "The end of the world is nigh, give me another subsidy so I can flush it down the toilet."'

'We intend to fly our way out of this crisis by giving passengers even more reasons to travel at even lower prices. I think a lot of airlines are making hay out of what happened and trying to create their own crisis. This is our chance to send out a clear message to the big, fat carriers who are looking for state subsidies. We're in the shit now. How are we going to dig our way out of it?'

'The only way to defeat terrorism here is not to be standing there whingeing with your aircraft on the ground looking for subsidies. It's to get there with lower fares and persuade people to travel more often. Despite the efforts of terrorists, normal life continues with millions of people travelling for normal leisure and business purposes. Our solution is to get back in the air with more passengers and lower fares. We will lose less money than we will by sitting on the ground and having the begging bowl out to the European Governments for massive amounts of money.'

Post-9/11: 'Somebody in the current market has to talk about expansion. A lot of the problems you see in the airline industry—let's take Aer Lingus as a classic example—are not because of the awful incidents in the US. These had been coming for many months and possibly years. Some of Europe's flag-carriers are still grossly overstaffed, they run at losses, they sell below cost and they're incredibly inefficient. They are nancy boys. A massive restructuring of those airlines is 20 years overdue. To listen to the flag-carriers, you'd think the end of the world is nigh. Well, we're making money.'

'I can guarantee you, we've had record bookings over this weekend. We're not going to be put out of business by a bunch of terrorists.'

'You might be scared of flying at £200 return, but you'll be a lot less scared flying at £20 return.'

'Drop your prices and you'll be amazed how demand comes back.'

'We lost a couple of million quid. It's Mickey Mouse money.'

'We do better in downturns than in periods of economic growth. Businesses trade down and get much more price-sensitive, which benefits us. Our biggest growth periods have been after September 11 and the Iraq war.'

On Irish Government measures to combat the risk of Severe Acute Respiratory Syndrome (SARS): 'At a time when Irish tourism is trying to fend off the adverse effects of the war in Iraq and the international economic downturn, we are now to be hindered by a bunch of incompetent civil servants designing irresponsible and unnecessary leaflets and passenger announcements solely to appear to the local media like they are actually doing something, instead of sensibly analysing and addressing the actual threat to Ireland or Irish people of SARS in a proportionate and realistic fashion. The non-existent threat to Ireland from SARS is a media invention which is in danger of running riot because of the absence of any common-sense response from panicked civil servants and spineless politicians. More people in Europe got killed falling off barstools this weekend than got killed from SARS. What's next, leaflets to warn visitors about the threat of Legionnaires' Disease in Irish hospitals? Why don't you get a grip of yourselves? We would appreciate it if the next time the Department of Transport wants to panic and pander to some manufactured media controversy, you might consider actually consulting with one or two airlines. I have never read such a ridiculous, spineless, load of nonsense.'

On the Foot-and-Mouth emergency: 'If you have a changeable ticket, you can change, we suffer the loss; if it's a non-changeable ticket and you have insurance, then you should be covered in most cases. If you took the decision to buy a non-refundable ticket and did not take out travel insurance, please don't come to us asking us to be the insurer of last resort because, I promise you, we have our own problems at the moment.'

On new UK security measures: 'These are farcical Keystone Kops security measures that don't add anything except to block up airports. These measures are giving the terrorists and extremists an unbelievable public relations success. We are not going to die at the hands of toiletries.'

'It feels like Laurel and bloody Hardy are working at the Department of Transport, coming up with these security measures. The western world is not in danger from lethal toiletries.'

'Searching terrorist suspects like five- and six-year-old children travelling with their parents and elderly people in wheelchairs going to Spain on holidays, who are clearly potentially a great threat to the great British public, will have the terrorists laughing in the caves in Pakistan. Look at what we can do with just a couple of mobile telephone calls.'

'You don't see the Government confiscating lipsticks and gel-filled bras on the London Underground. Most of them couldn't identify a gel-filled bra if it jumped up and bit them anyway. Ladies' padded bras with gel inside are not weapons of mass destruction. It's simply a way of politicians making it look like they are doing something.'

'These restrictions have absolutely no impact on security, they are nonsensical and the height of stupidity, but the more you call these restrictions stupid and nonsensical the more the UK Department of Transport digs its heels in and says, "Oh, we have to protect the nation, this is needed for security." If it was, they would apply these restrictions on more likely terrorist targets, like the London Underground or Eurotunnel. If you look at where the terrorists have been striking in recent years, it's the London Underground and the trains in Madrid.'

'The way to defeat the extremists is to return air travel to normal. The sooner the Government returns the London airports and British air travel to normal, the sooner the growth in air travel can continue. It is unfair to blame BAA for the massive security disruptions of last weekend. It was the Government who quadrupled the required security checks and yet failed to provide additional army and police personnel to enable this fourfold increase to be carried out. What the Government should then have done was return air travel to normality in much the same way as it successfully restored normal operations to the London Underground within two days of the 7/7 attacks.'

'This country is in danger of being taken over by 'securocrats' who seem intent on bringing airports to a grinding halt. These are the same people who came up with the ridiculous idea that stopping people travelling with toothpaste and eye make-up would make us safer.'

'We are now reaching a point where security people don't want to do the overtime. Security experts tell us that staff are getting tired and that their attention to detail is now diminishing rapidly. The reality is, there is no heightened security. The Government tried to get our European partners to adopt the reduced luggage allowances and they told us to go away.'

'The way to defeat terrorism is, one, to arrest the bloody terrorists, and, two, keep the system working normally.'

On a bomb scare in Scotland: 'The police force were outstanding in their field. But all they did was stand in their field. They kept passengers on board while they played with a suspect package for 2¾ hours. Extraordinary.'

On a Sunday afternoon when only 7 out of 14 security check-points at Stansted Airport were manned: 'The only explanation was that Arsenal and Tottenham Hotspur were both playing football on the television and there were huge no-shows among security staff because many of them live in North London. We have written to the Football League asking them not to schedule Arsenal and Spurs matches on the same Sunday afternoon.'

'Air marshals are a complete waste of time. I can't think of anything that would reduce security more than having a guy on board with a gun.'

POLITICIANS

'I think we did make a mistake with the Sarkozy advert, but only because it wasn't particularly funny. I'm available to kiss and make up with Mrs Sarkozy any time she wants.'

'I upset a lot of people because I tell them what I think. I'm disrespectful towards what is perceived to be authority. Like, I think the Prime Minister of Ireland is a gobshite, because he won't make a decision. Two years he's been promising us a second terminal at Dublin, and nothing's happened. Nobody ever takes on Governments. Everyone wants to work their way round them with influence and lobbying. Why not shout the bastards down?'

On Bertie Ahern: 'Only in "Bertie's Blunderland" are passengers faced with queuing to get into Ireland's main airport, as well as to get out of it. Competition works. Ryanair works. Ahern's transport policy clearly doesn't. From the M50, where the cars don't fit, to the port tunnel, where trucks don't fit, to Dublin Airport, where sadly nothing fits, this Government has repeatedly failed the Irish people. We've had a clown as Taoiseach for the past 10 years.'

'We've had inefficiency, fudge, dither and buying off the public sector. The reason the health service is in shit is because we've had no leadership in this country for the last 10 years. The road transport is a mess, public transport is a mess, because of everything that's been done by Bertie.'

'I was listening to all this crap about the great job he has done for the economy. Bertie Ahern has been a disaster for the Irish economy for the last 10 years. We have a Government of lemmings, led by the biggest lemming of all, who is incapable of making a long-term strategic decision. The next Government is going to have to deal with some really harsh realities. That eejit hasn't got any bit of leadership, any bit of foresight, any principle on which he will stand up and be counted. He is fundamentally spineless and follows the line of least resistance.'

'It's called democracy. If the Prime Minister is incompetent or doing a shit job, I or every other citizen of this country am free to call him a spineless tosser, which is what he is.'

On being asked to meet Bertie Ahern to resolve an airport strike: 'We got a call from the Taoiseach's office asking us to enter talks with the union. We said, "Fuck off and open the airport." It was his job to keep the fucking airport open. There was nothing he could do, it was very tense, very difficult circumstances. So we said, "Tell him to send in the army and open the fucking airport." The only thing that Bertie wanted on the Sunday when the airport was closed was for me to come down to Government Buildings at six o'clock. He wanted me there in time for the TV news, so that the message would be "O'Leary summoned to Government Buildings for crisis talks." So I said, "No, fuck off. Go fucking open the airport.""

'I don't want to meet the Taoiseach. All I want is a decision out of the bugger. I haven't met him for two years. We strongly oppose Bertie and his fudgemeisters in the Cabinet. There are muppets in the Government who had failed to achieve anything over the past decade. Bertie's exam results will read "F" for failing to keep his promises and "F" for failing to keep his deadlines.'

'A hundred and something 80-year-olds were able to get together and elect a new pope in 24 hours but Bertie Ahern has been dithering about a new terminal for the past three years. As a result, Dublin Airport is not just a slum, it is a testament to the failure of Bertie Ahern to keep his own election promises. Another terminal provided by the same people who brought us the Black Hole of Calcutta is not competition, it's still the Black Hole of Calcutta. The Government has been forced to open up telecoms, electricity and other sectors to competition, and airports shouldn't be any different. Competition works, but Bertie giving in to his buddies in the trade unions doesn't.'

'You expect Bertie Ahern to stand up for something. What does he make a stand on? Smoking in pubs! Why? Because the unions support it, that's why.'

On being accused of 'tooth-and-claw capitalism' by Bertie Ahern: 'It was a political speech made to a trade union audience, so what would you expect?'

'Unlike Irish politicians we don't accept cash—only credit cards.'

On Bertie's successor: 'Brian Cowen couldn't be any worse; I think he'll be significantly better than Bertie Ahern, but that's not setting the bar very high.'

On Minister Mary O'Rourke: 'She's an idiot. I'm very supportive of people who come from the Midlands but I'm not supportive of an idiot no matter where they come from. Most politicians are idiots, but if you look on the scale of idiocy she'd be right up there at the top. She was a woeful Minister. She had to be put in her box. I would have to ask why you would let a schoolteacher run such an important ministerial portfolio? I hope she goes to Education or Health, where they deserve her. Mary O'Rourke says she doesn't mind criticism but, in reality, she's thin-skinned. She's out of her depth in her job and she can't take the flak that goes with that. It's been a sequence of disasters since the day she took power. She's been in the job four years and what's happened? We've ended years of tourism growth and lurched from one crisis to the next. She can dish it out but can't take it. Politicians are there to be slagged off, particularly if they're as incompetent as she is. She's a *Yes, Minister* character, a Sir Humphrey who cannot make any decent decisions for herself and the Minister for Monopolies. Mary O'Rourke and her pals in Aer Rianta are the only ones objecting to what we are offering. What we are dealing with here is a Monty-Python-type Minister from Athlone who just keeps saying no, no, no. It's the Athlone voodoo school of economics. This will take me off Mary O'Rourke's Christmas card list.'

'Any time politicians get involved in an industry or regulating an industry, they fuck it up. It's what they do best.'

'I have never yet come across a politician who will make a political decision in your favour or against your favour unless it was in their interest, or in what they consider to be the national interest. They just don't make decisions based on the fact that you sponsored something, or that they stayed in some holiday home of yours.'

On political donations: 'If the party is going down the right road we should try and support it. The only two parties I wouldn't give a contribution to would be Sinn Féin and Labour. Sinn Féin are a bunch of mindless morons and they have the economic policies of a two-year-old. Labour have my sympathies, but that'd be about the height of it.'

On making any donations to any political party: 'That's my business and none of yours.'

'Why don't bloody politicians stop subsidising fucking industry?'

'The whole purpose of regulators is to be a convenient political cover for the lack of political will to allow competition. And so what the politicians say is, "Well, this is a natural monopoly, therefore we're going to impose a regulator and he's going to protect the consumer interest." And what happens from the second after the regulator's imposed is the regulated monopoly starts gaming him.'

On the Irish Aviation Regulator: 'He has no credibility as an independent regulator and it is time he resigned or was dismissed. He is a regulatory poodle, a spineless woolly lamb, rubber-stamping unjustified price increases and double-charging at the Government-owned DAA Monopoly. The airport users were denied access to what the airport's costs were based on, and it's very hard to justify a 300% increase in any cost over a three-year period, and that's what's happened with check-in charges. So far we've won one case and lost about six. We think there is a very good chance of success in this case; this case is much more blatant. We will continue to judicially review every single decision he makes while this is the quality of the regulatory process in this country. He's limp-wristed and lacking spine. What you would expect from a civil servant? I am not surprised to be in his bold-boys list. I have written to the Transport Department to ask for him to be dismissed.'

To the assistant secretary of the Department of Transport: 'As the supposed senior civil servant with responsibility, you continue to use weasel words in dealing with our reasonable complaints.'

On Irish Government plans to fine airlines who bring asylum-seekers to Ireland: 'I would be surprised if they stopped one person using this method. If people want to come, they will come using false papers. It's not up to us to stop them. It's politically vacuous and nonsensical.'

'This Government cannot fix the roads, railways or Luas before returning to the country in three or four years, but it can fix air access, tourism and the restaurants, hotels and bars. However, you must get off your backsides now and get it done. It needs decisions and action.'

'It has been suggested that more car parks and cars are against Government policy. I am not sure about that. Over the last five years I have discovered that more tourists and lower-cost access into this country is also against Government policy.'

On presenting to a Dáil Committee: 'I will stay here all evening. There is no time pressure. I will keep going,

Chairman. I will try to speed up the answers. You tell me when to stop.'

On mistaking the name of an Irish TD: 'It was the Saddam-like moustache that confused me.'

'I think the most influential person in Europe in the last 20 to 30 years has been Margaret Thatcher, who has left a lasting legacy that has driven us towards lower taxes and greater efficiency. And without her we'd all be living in some French bloody inefficient unemployed republic.'

On flying Tony Blair on his holidays to Carcassonne: 'The savings the Blair family made flying with us compared to flying with British Airways to Toulouse were in excess of £2,000. Even for the most well-off people these are huge savings which simply cannot be ignored. Even very rich people, who may be travelling with four or five children and a nanny, are turning to us to save money. Even Tony Blair doesn't get paid enough for British Airways fares.'

On Gordon Brown: 'He just raised taxes on airlines. It has fuck-all to do with climate change. We've written several letters to the UK Treasury, asking what the money's going to be spent on. We still haven't gotten a reply. This is the problem with all this environmental claptrap. It's a convenient excuse for politicians to just start taxing people. Some of these guilt-laden, middle-class liberals think it's somehow good: "Oh, that's my contribution to the environment." It's not. You're just being robbed. It's just highway fucking robbery.'

On David Cameron: 'If I were him I would stop competing over who is better at riding a bicycle and call for a serious debate on the next generation of nuclear power stations. Sticking a windmill on top of your house is not the answer.'

'Politicians call them eco-taxes, but that's just spin—it's just taking more money off us. David Cameron may be holidaying in Cornwall but he flew halfway round the world just to see some huskies. David Cameron can hug trees because he won't have to do much to get into power, but it is not a way to run a country. Gordon Brown is only staying in Britain because he is too frightened that if he leaves someone will nick his job. It's just Government by poll and spin-doctor. Thatcher and Blair didn't dither, they just made their decisions. Where do all these carbon offsets go? Corrupt African dictatorships and staff in New York. The money doesn't actually go to planting trees. The green lobby are like those old guys in the medieval market-place, shouting about the end of the world. Climate change is not the biggest threat to mankind. If it is, why is the summer so crappy?'

On Charlie Haughey: 'Bring back Charlie. He may have been crooked but at least he got things done.'

THE EUROPEAN COMMISSION

'Sometimes it's good to show Brussels the two fingers.'

'Consumers have been ripped off for the past 50 years because Governments got together with the airlines after 1945. British Airways got the monopoly in the UK, Air France the monopoly in France and Lufthansa the monopoly in Germany. The airline industry is the only industry where the producers are allowed by the idiots in Brussels to get together once or twice a year to fix the fares and route capacities and they get anti-trust immunity to do it. It's a joke.'

'I think we should blow the place up and shoot all the regulators and the airline business might actually prosper. I've no intention of making life easy for bureaucrats.'

'It's fun to challenge the European Commission because they are politically corrupt.'

'Bureaucrats in Brussels have been blathering on about European unity for ages but the low-cost airlines are at the forefront of delivering it. We are the means by which hundreds of thousands can now travel back and forth; they are almost commuting.'

'I believe these morons in the European Commission are making air travel more expensive, but I wouldn't be interested in sitting down trying to educate a bunch of civil servants.'

'The European Transport Commissioner, Jacques Barrot in Brussels, is smart, but his assistants are real idiots. We have an education process to do on the Commission.'

On an EU investigation into subsidies at Charleroi Airport: 'The arrangements we have at Charleroi Airport are competitive, non-discriminatory and available to all. Ryanair have no concern about any formal or informal inquiries made by the EU into our successful operations are Brussels Charleroi. Someone here is looking for a smoking gun and there isn't one. We haven't received a letter from the EU, but if we do I think it would get a pretty short reply. I think it would consist of two words: Foxtrot Oscar. We have spent much more than we have ever received from the Walloon region. We spent over €100 million building the bloody base. We created their airport from nothing. So our reply will say, "We're paying nothing, love Mick."'

On a delayed EU ruling on Charleroi Airport: 'Part of the difficulty is the share price. We're a publicly owned company and we're dying with a thousand cuts here. Frankly, if the decision is going to be negative, will you just publish the fucking thing and then let's deal with it as best we can.'

On an adverse EU ruling on Charleroi Airport: 'It's a complete fuck-up which is going to overturn 20 years of competition in air travel, but it wouldn't be the first time the EU has made a balls of an investigation. It looks like the EU are trying to come up with some communist rules, which means that everyone pays the same high costs and charges the same high fares. This is an attack not just on Ryanair but on the entire low-fares sector. We consider this a disaster for consumers. The judgment is just blindingly wrong. There will be a repayment over my dead body. We have written back to say fuck off.'

'There are fucking Kim Il-Jungs in the Commission. You cannot have civil servants trying to design rules that make everything a level playing field. That's called North fucking Korea, and everybody is starving there. It's only in communist Europe where the Commission can't even run its own bloody budget would they dream of telling ordinary people to pay higher fares so we can have some mythical level playing field. They are pursuing some form of communist fucking Valhalla.'

'This Communist intervention has fucked the publicly-owned airports. The impression given by the Kim Il-Jungs on the Commission is that we jackboot the shit out of Charleroi. The truth is that Charleroi is profitable, we are net payers to the airport, and it has to compete. At any given time we have five or six airports falling over themselves to take the business.'

'Are we the good guys? Absolutely. Are the Commission the bad guys? They are the evil empire if this is the kind of decision they come up with. Brussels is the centre of communist Europe.'

'Would it have made a difference if anyone else had made the case to Brussels? No. It wouldn't matter who it was with those Communists on the Commission. Zey are Communists, numbnuts, bureaucrats. Ve vill fight zem in ze hills, ve vill fight zem on ze beaches, ve vill neverrrr zurrenderr. Our lawyers are so confident of winning it on appeal, I'm worried.'

'Part of the problem is that this was a case of one half of Belgium, the one that owns Brussels Zaventem, the city's main airport, suing the other bit that owns Charleroi. The Belgians handled it ineptly. The Belgian Commissioner didn't know whether he was coming or going.'

'There is going to be a permanent smell hanging over us.'

'Before Ryanair arrived, Charleroi's baggage handlers were paid to sit around like the local job centre. Now two million people a year fly there and it's booming. Ryanair has never received a subsidy. The money we received from Charleroi was money we paid them in the first place. We paid the published charges and they kicked back 90%. We pass that on to the public. We give the public what it fucking wants. The EU Commission said this ruling will increase fares. In the United States that would cause a riot. That is how lunatic this decision is. It is bizarre.'

'Why should a Wal-Mart located outside a city centre, for example, pay the same rent as those in city-centre locations? It's like saying that Wal-Mart will only get the same discounts as the corner grocery store, and if Wal-Mart asks for any discounts on bigger volumes they will be told no.'

'We don't accept that we have received any state aid at Charleroi Airport. All we received were discounts, just like Tesco would receive from its cheese suppliers. You would not see the Commission interfering in the discounts that supermarkets such as Tesco negotiate to bring lower prices to consumers. It's impossible to envisage the Commission preventing McDonald's negotiating discounts from its suppliers to lower the cost of its meals to consumers. Why should the Commission do it to us?'

'Some people love the idea that the Charleroi decision is going to end low-cost air travel for ever. It isn't—we are an unstoppable force.'

'This is either the dawn of a new era in low-cost travel or it is a death sentence. The Commission may well be about to turn back the clock and say, "Sorry but we don't want low fares." The loss here will not be Ryanair's but consumers'. We don't want to go back to an era of high fares for rich people. You can't go back to the days when people paid five or six hundred quid a ticket. There is no compromise. We're not changing the cost base at Brussels Charleroi by one cent or one centime. We're off to the courts.'

'We are not going to be shouldered with stupid legislation coming out of Brussels which has no effect but to make air travel less competitive. No bureaucrat or Brussels lobbyist is going to block Ryanair's business model. If it does, we're off to the European court. We're not going to let this one drop and we'll be off to every European court in every hill and valley. We will never surrender. The Commission's decision on Charleroi is crucial. It will be our Waterloo and we will win it. We will sue the arse off the Commission.'

'We will lose a lot of these cases, then win them all on appeal. Our appeal is a legal case: it won't require lobbying politicians, who are as useful as condoms in a convent. The Commission will have to prove the unprovable.'

'Given our outstanding record with legal actions we're very confident we'll be successful. So far the tally's running at 99 losses and two wins.'

'We're here to fight. As Churchill said, "In defeat, defiance."'

'We've got €1.2 billion in cash. The interest from next week's deposit will pay whatever the bloody fine is. The issue here is the principle.'

'Undoubtedly there are people I irritate, who find me feisty and confrontational. Will there be some people out there who believe that my performance or my handling of the Charleroi case hasn't contributed or has caused a negative decision in the case? Yes, I'm sure there are. I think that if we lose that case, ultimately the responsibility rests with me. And it would be up to the board and the shareholders. If they want to change me, they can change me any time. I accept that some people may question my performance, but I think I am happy to stand over it.'

On European air traffic control: 'Deregulate and privatise the fuckers and let them compete.'

'Air traffic control can walk out any time they like and no one gets compensation. Public officials shouldn't be able to go on strike. They can't be sacked, so there should be some quid pro quo.'

'I don't give a damn about labour laws in France. We'll break the laws in France if that's what needs to be done.'

On EU Commissioner Neelie Kroes' approval of an Alitalia/Air One merger: 'She'll be rolling over like a poodle having her tummy tickled and rubber-stamping the thing. We think the EU Commission is biased against us, but then we would say that, wouldn't we?'

'We're not paranoid but Brussels really do have it in for us.'

'We will be complying with European legislation pledging compensation for passenger delays but not embracing them. It's a lot of rubbish. They will get overturned in the end. It's stupid legislation but that is what Brussels does. Most claims will be met with "Not our fault, go away." It's just a bullshit piece of legislation and it won't survive a case in the European Court.'

AER LINGUS

'Our forthcoming charitable work may include a sneak preview of the Aer Lingus calendar with some granny in a swimsuit.'

'Aer Lingus is basically the same as Ryanair, except it's twice the price.'

On Aer Lingus being named best-value airline in Europe in a survey: 'In reality Aer Lingus have won an award for ripping people off by slightly less than they were ripping people off years ago.'

'Europe is miles bigger than the Ireland-England routes. In Europe there are high fares that even make Aer Lingus look cheap.'

'Aer Lingus has been transformed in the past 12 months by following exactly what we were doing five and 10 years ago.'

'We carry four times the traffic Aer Lingus does with half the staff.'

'On the question as to whether we are in bed with Aer Lingus at Dublin Airport, the only area where we are in negotiations with Aer Lingus is in relation to our proposal for the competing second terminal at Dublin Airport. We are not in talks with Aer Lingus on anything else.'

After 9/11: 'This is not a good time for airlines like Aer Lingus, not because of terrorist attacks, but because they are mismanaged. If Aer Lingus pulls transatlantic routes or goes bankrupt, we will look seriously at it. We'd make sure that the services were provided from Ireland to the us by an Irish company. The bottom has fallen out of the American tourist market for the moment.'

When referring to a male Aer Lingus trade union executive: 'Darling.'

To Willie Walsh, then ceo of Aer Lingus: 'As we confirmed to the Advertising Standards Authority, we would be delighted to run ads detailing your actual average fares when Aer Lingus publishes audited accounts that set out this sectoral information. If you and your fellow directors wish to hide the numbers in your annual accounts, you can't complain subsequently that those same accounts give rise to numbers which aren't precisely accurate. Aer Lingus is still a high-fares airline, it will always be a high-fares airline, although at least under your new management team, it is a better-run high-fares airline than it was in the past. Give me a call if Aer Lingus wants to provide transparent air fare and customer service numbers on a regular basis as Ryanair does.'

On Willie Walsh's departure from Aer Lingus: 'The chief executive of Aer Lingus is no great fan or friend of Ryanair. He will be fried alive if he takes us on in Europe. We have dug a graveyard for his competitors, having already seen off Go, Jetmagic and Jetgreen. Every muttonhead in Dublin will be willing to waste their money dreaming dreams. There is plenty of cash out there looking for the flavour of the day. He's done an outstanding job, but anyone who thinks Aer Lingus is a low-cost airline is smoking dope. I blame this pudding of a Government for losing him. It shows astonishing incompetence. Their decisions are as rare as snow in the Sahara.'

On the resignation of his senior Finance Manager to become Chief Financial Officer of Aer Lingus: 'I wouldn't call him high-level management, he was more mid-level. He's a good guy and we'll be sorry to lose him but we have four people in here who could fill his job by lunchtime. We have a senior management team of 10 and a second tier of 40. He was one of the 40. He is going to the wrong place. We are pleased to see Aer Lingus recruit some decent management.'

On the privatisation of Aer Lingus: 'What you are going to privatise is something that the Government still hopes to control in some kind of completely screwed-up way. If you want to privatise it, privatise the bloody thing and get the hell out of it.'

On Ryanair acquiring 29% of Aer Lingus: 'We first discussed the prospect of buying shares in Aer Lingus the Tuesday evening before it floated on the stock market on Wednesday. So it's happened that quickly. That's why nothing leaked. Because we weren't discussing it for yonks. At Ryanair we don't sit around agonising over things.'

'This merger also provides Aer Lingus with a secure long-term future as part of one strong Irish airline group, whereas, on its own, we believe it is doomed to a bleak future as a small, regional, high-cost airline which recorded dismal financial results. If Aer Lingus turns down our offer, they are going to find themselves in five years' time as an eight-million-passenger airline competing with an 80-million-passenger airline next door. Our offer embarrassed the board of Aer Lingus. Five days earlier they were happy to sell the business at €2.20 a share, then they were trying to justify rejecting our offer of €2.80. But it's not a matter for the management or board; it's a matter for shareholders. Aer Lingus has discovered this new strategy of splendid isolation. The last time that was tried was by Éamon de Valera after the war and it led to 40 years of economic stagnation. I'd suggest Aer Lingus is doomed to a similar failure.'

'There aren't other opportunities in an industry that we know well and have a lot of competence in, and in a company which has a high cost base where we could reduce the cost base and fares in relatively short order. I can find much cheaper ways of making mischief than spending €204 million. I wouldn't call them a low-fares airline, nor a success. We think that the Government would quite enjoy working closely with a joint Ryanair-Aer Lingus group to develop Irish tourism through lower air fares.'

'I am happy for the Irish Government to be a significant minority shareholder in Aer Lingus.'

'Helping Aer Lingus to improve its cost base and efficiency to increase profits is better use of our spare cash than putting it on deposit.'

'We have no plans other than to work with the existing Aer Lingus management to continue the policies followed by Aer Lingus management over the last few years.'

One week later: 'Who said we weren't going to do anything radical? There is enormous scope for cost reduction here—85% of Aer Lingus traffic is in the same markets as Ryanair. Its unit costs are more than double Ryanair's. How much fat do you think there is in there?'

'There is no doubt there would be significant job losses at Aer Lingus if the Ryanair bid is successful because that is one of the ways to reduce costs. We won't just be trimming costs, we will be slashing them. There is schiz-ophrenia in the Aer Lingus model and we would make that schizophrenia even more defined by significantly lowering the short-haul fares and by significantly improving the long-haul product and service. Let's face it, that wouldn't be too difficult. We would not be talking about trimmings, we would be talking about slashings in the amount of waste in Aer Lingus's short-haul operation, which is enormous. The old restrictive work practices, all that sitting around on their hands, will all change.'

'In the last four weeks Aer Lingus management appear to have made little progress on their cost reduction plan, beyond changing its name. Their 'customer driven plan with a clear business focus' is Japanese for higher fares.'

On possible job losses at Aer Lingus: 'Tough shit.'

On Aer Lingus Director and former Anglo-Irish Bank chief executive Sean Fitzpatrick: 'Mr Fitzpatrick acquired only 9,090 Aer Lingus shares at a cost of just €20,000, which is less than one-seventh of his current investment of 15,000 Ryanair shares, which are valued at over €140,000. We commend Mr S. Fitzpatrick for his proven track record in backing winners.'

'The EU Commission's decision to prohibit this merger between two EU airlines which between them represent just 5% of European airline traffic is not just unprecedented but, in our view, unlawful. We call on the commission to explain how it can rubber-stamp mergers between larger airlines such as Air France/KLM, Lufthansa/ Swiss and Lufthansa/Austrian, when these Airlines have bigger positions at their home airports than the combined Ryanair/Aer Lingus share at Dublin Airport. There's no question of relinquishing our shares.'

'The prohibition of Ryanair's bid for Aer Lingus, which guaranteed over €100 million per annum in passenger savings, was a biased, politically motivated, anti-consumer decision. We again call on the European Commission to end this politically corrupt bias. It is quite clear that European consumers can't trust this Commission. It supports mergers which result in higher fares and surcharges. It's a nakedly political decision. This is designed to appeal solely to the narrow vested interests of the Irish Government. Aer Lingus passengers should send the bill for their higher fares and fuel surcharges to the European Commission in Brussels.'

'If I stood buck naked in the street, I don't think Brussels would look more favourably on Ryanair's bid for Aer Lingus. It would be easier for a camel to pass through the eye of a needle than for Ryanair to get a fair hearing in Brussels.'

On not attending an Aer Lingus Extraordinary General Meeting: 'I would have very little to learn at the EGM of a high-fares airline like Aer Lingus.'

On Aer Lingus' failure to hold an EGM: 'Ryanair could then convene the EGM itself and any cost incurred by Ryanair must be discharged by Aer Lingus and deducted from Aer Lingus' director fees. I can envisage booking out the Four Seasons or perhaps the Shelbourne Hotel with a free bar for the Aer Lingus EGM, with the Aer

Lingus directors personally meeting the expense. One can but dream.'

'Aer Lingus are trying to force us to sell our stake and they have no hope of success. They're only doing that to distract the attention of their shareholders away from how badly the company is run. We will buy Aer Lingus eventually just as all small airlines like TAP, Olympic, Clickair, Vueling and Air Berlin will be bought up.'

'If someone wants to offer us a big return on our 25% stake, we're always happy to talk to anyone. I don't suspect there will be many takers.'

'I'm celebrating the fall in value in our investment in Aer Lingus. It's an accurate response to the management's current performance. Aer Lingus is likely to be taken over and the most likely candidate to take over Aer Lingus is Ryanair, because frankly nobody else has any interest in taking over Aer Lingus. It's too small and too high-cost to survive as an independent airline.'

On a €90-million write-down on the value of the Aer Lingus stake: 'The actual write-down would be a lot lower. I'd certainly be very surprised if the values got up above the level of what we paid for it, so you're probably looking at a write down of some kind. Even if it was €90 million we wouldn't be losing any sleep over it. In fact I'd be happy to take a €90 million write down if it meant that Aer Lingus' share price was averaging €1.90. We said it was going nowhere without our bid and the state of the share price makes that obvious.'

On whether the large write-down was a good use of Ryanair shareholders' money: 'Yes, and you can attribute that to Ryanair's largest individual shareholder. It has been mentioned by our shareholders: the response was two words, and the second word was "off". It is in the national interest for us to help out our national airline. The €300 million invested by Ryanair in Aer Lingus is just a drop in the ocean. This isn't a lot of money. I sit in front of our shareholders and say, "I own more shares in the company than you do, now fuck off.'"

BRITISH AIRWAYS

'British Airways are skyway robbery.'

'I have no time for large airlines who say they care and then screw you for six or seven hundred quid almost every time you fly. Businessmen now need to be competitive. They need to stop drinking champagne at six o'clock in the morning on British Airways flights. They need to get there on time. With Ryanair statistically you're more on time. Why the hell would anyone fly with BA and pay four or five hundred quid just to be late?'

'The idea that you get on board a seven o'clock flight from Brussels to Frankfurt and you get some inedible breakfast and two screw-top bottles of champagne that you can't drink anyway, that's over.'

'You're always going to be delayed on British Airways. You'll get crap food and a free drink worth £2 and you're going to pay £400 for it. The era of these rip-off airlines and horrible wine you can't even drink are over.'

'British Airways tried rubbishing our service and when

that failed the last thing left was to send in lawyers. We did have problems but they are sorted. What frills do you get on BA? Old aircraft. Crap seating. They screw you for a high fare, serve you with reheated crap you would never eat in a roadside cafe, and you notionally get free drink you have actually paid for 40 times.'

'BA have been going downhill for years. I don't think they have the right management. Bob Ayling has long stopped pulling his weight. It is ridiculous you have to pay £200 on a BA flight to have a gin and tonic. It has been over-charging for years. Especially on its overseas flights.'

'British Airways keep turning passengers away with fuel surcharge after fuel surcharge, high fares, poor punctu-ality, flight cancellations and no catering. At least on Ryanair, customers can buy a sandwich with £100 they have saved over BA's high fares.'

On passengers stranded in a BA strike: 'This punctured the myth that BA has tried to perpetuate that if something goes wrong BA will look after you. Thousands of BA's high-fares passengers are left to sleep on the terminal floor with no free food, no free drinks and no hotel accommodation. They left the passengers in the terminal for the weekend. By the way, we probably would too if we had that bad a weekend. You can't buy 80,000 hotel rooms.'

'As the British Airways strike at Heathrow confirmed, the service that high-fares airline provide when things go wrong is no different to that provided by low-fares carriers.'

'On British Airways, your luggage will travel further than you will.'

On cancelling his £900 ticket to Milan on British Airways, booked by his investment bankers, in preference for a £59 ticket on his own airline: 'It just shows you how banks piss away money. No, I didn't get a £59 fare because I'm the chief executive, anyone could have booked with us today and got that—it's midweek, a quiet time and we do one-way pricing.'

'I am saving European air travellers hundreds of millions of pounds every year over the airfares they would have paid to British Airways. We're in this business to drive fares down, really rub it in the noses of BA and highlight that BA are ripping you off.'

'I see myself as a jumped-up Paddy running a good airline that gives great fares and screws BA.'

'We declared that we were going to smash the BA monopoly of high fares on short-haul European routes; that we have clearly done. British Airways just cannot compete with us in the short-haul market and there is not a lot they can do about it.'

'If British Airways wants a price war with Ryanair then they should just name the time and place. If they want a war, they have come to the right place. We have the financial clout to be able to do this. We do not operate the same way as BA. There is no con.'

On hanging a promotional seat sale banner outside the British Airways flight shop in Piccadilly, London: 'We're doing this to re-emphasise Ryanair's position as Europe's low-fares carrier.'

'We are determined to drive prices ever lower, by a half within five years, and last year we carried 20% for free. What's BA's response been? Well, last week they said they would introduce new uniforms. It's back to the Fifties, which is where most of these muttonheads' thinking is. If fine wine and food don't get you and Heathrow doesn't persuade you, now you have got shorter skirts to attract you back to BA and its £200 average fares, or four times higher than ours. In five or 10 years they'll be flying as few as 10 short-haul flights into Heathrow or maybe Gatwick. If I were the chief executive of BA, I would give up.'

'Why don't British Airways reduce other costs instead of always gouging their passengers? While oil prices have doubled, BA fuel surcharges have gone up twelvefold. BA and other airlines are simply using oil price increases to jack up fares.'

'British Airways won't be growing its existing emission levels because it's going nowhere—it's shrinking. A move to the moon might be needed to streamline British Airway's operations.'

'There is too much "We really admire our competitors." All bollocks. Everyone wants to kick the shit out of everyone else. We want to beat the crap out of British Airways. They mean to kick the crap out of us.'

'We love tilting at the English, have done it for about 700 years, but we're only getting our own back. Remember they beat the crap out of us for the first 600.'

On his recreations as listed in Who's Who: 'BA-bashing.'

'British Airways did not think we could afford to fight them in court. It is an age-old dirty trick by BA. But we did fight them and we won. It's game, set and match to us. I would like to thank BA for taking this action to prove what everybody already knows—that they are expensive. These bully-boy tactics are typical of BA, and the attempt to gag Ryanair or frighten the national newspapers was doomed to failure.'

'Too many airlines that have gotten it right for a certain amount of time have then suddenly started thinking they can walk on water, so they start buying hotels, or expanding into other businesses, or—if you look at British Airways—trying to serve every market you can from Britain.'

'Someone has to persuade the British Airways workforce the way forward is being more efficient and more productive. Two years ago their check-in staff walked off the job when they weren't even on strike; it was Gate Gourmet staff who were. If they'd have done that at Ryanair they wouldn't have come back. The staff have something like an average of 12 days off ill a year with built-in extra days? At Ryanair it's three days.'

'There are times when it's justified to go on strike over pay, but it's insane to do so at an airline as financially troubled as British Airways.'

When British Airways began its own low-fares airline Go: 'They must be smoking too much dope. It's a rubbish airline that's not worth anything. If they pay us to take it off their hands, we will. We could not afford to buy Go because the damage to our earnings and profitability would be huge.'

'British Airways has no fucking idea how to run a low-fare airline like Go. I know more about flying on Concorde than Bob Ayling does about running a low-cost airline, and I've never flown on Concorde.'

'Before Go the airline industry was run by a dodgy Greek and a Paddy.'

On the former Go Chief Executive: 'She's the fragrant Barbara Cassani. I'd advise her to shut up, take the money, be very happy that she's one of the very few people who made a lot of money out of aviation. easyJet paid far too much for Go. I don't think we can call Barbara an entrepreneur. The only time she competed with Ryanair in Ireland, she lasted four months. That's why she is writing books and we are running Europe's most successful and profitable airline.'

On fighting Go on the Dublin–Edinburgh route: 'This is going to be a disaster for Go because if the best they can manage is £45 as against our £29 nobody will flying with Go except for the passengers they take off Aer Lingus. At these prices Go doesn't even qualify as a low-fares airline. While we welcome the competition, I don't think we'll notice them, but they will notice us. Their schedule is crap. Their first flight out in the morning is at 10 a.m. We will be out and back at that stage—goodbye Go.'

'I can't for the life of me think why BA would take over KLM. KLM is a basket case. BA is a basket case too. You put the two together and you get an even bigger basket case. With BA and KLM's deep pockets, Go and Buzz could sell tickets at a loss to drive carriers like us, with no rich parent to call on, from certain air routes. While we are keen to take on Goliath, we want a fair fight.'

After 9/11: 'British Airways should have sacked half the management on 12 September; instead they are all wandering around like masters of the universe. And they should have cut travel agents' commission. If you listened to them, you would swear the American Airlines deal was going to rescue their arse. It's not.'

'Do you know how many people British Airways has in its customer services department? 200. Do you know how many we have? Four.'

'BA's had a policy over the last few years of operating smaller aircraft, carrying fewer passengers and charging higher fares. I think it would be glaringly self-evident to a four-year-old where that policy has gone wrong. It's nuts. I'm quite pleased BA is doing the Fortnum and Mason strategy. We're happy doing the Tesco one.'

'BA will become the first company in economic history to make money by selling fewer things to fewer people at lower prices. It has no chance of working.'

'The more British Airways cuts back, the more we get to carry the great unwashed. We're not proud. It's bye-bye BA.'

'Go to BA headquarters and tell Rod Eddington he's going to grow profits by 12% this year and he'd have an orgasm. I say, Godspeed. You're doing an outstanding job. Keep it up.'

'We don't need BA to fall over itself for us to succeed. It's been falling over for the last five years.'

'We're asking British Airways whether they are prepared to give their "world's favourite airline" tag to a poor bunch of Paddies. We are going to borrow the BA advertising slogan as "the world's favourite airline", put a line through BA and say, "Oh no you are not—the Paddies are."'

'We will make Ryanair—a small, some would say, Mickey Mouse, Paddy airline—the largest airline in the world. We already have the advertising campaign ready which says "Ryanair, the World's Favourite Airline" since British Airways will no longer be able to use it in two years' time.'

'We fly to more destinations in Europe from London than British Airways. We carry more passengers from London to Europe than British Airways. In every market in which we compete with it, we out-carry British Airways, the world's favourite airline. In many respects, it is remarkable for a small Irish airline to be able to out-carry what is perceived to be the world's largest and favourite airline. British Airways is not even London's favourite airline—Ryanair is.'

'A Mickey Mouse Irish airline can start in a field in Waterford and in 20 years the self-styled, self-proclaimed world's favourite airline is overtaken by the world's lowest-price airline. Now there's a thing.'

'We will attack whoever is out there. We have spent the past couple of years attacking British Airways. Attacking BA is like kicking a dead sheep—there is not much point any more. We need to have someone to attack. It is always helpful to have an enemy out there.'

LUFTHANSA

'We are stuffing it to Lufty.'

'The Chief Executive of Lufthansa says Germans don't like low fares. How the fuck does he know? He's never offered them any. He is 18 months behind the times.'

'If €99 fares is the best Lufthansa can do for the World Cup then they shouldn't bother leaving the changing rooms. Their €99 fares are own goals. I feel like the Michael Owen of the airline industry, beating the Germans on their home turf.'

'Lufthansa in Germany makes even British Airways look cheap.'

'I'd like to thank Lufthansa for their help setting us up in Germany.'

'Lufthansa are using chapters one and two of the big airlines' book on how to stamp out competition. All they're trying to do is keep us tied up in the courts for a couple of months because they know that if they can head us off for the first few months we'll never get these new routes off the ground. Lufthansa went to a court in Cologne where it can get these things done at nine o'clock on a Friday night by convincing some dotty old judge that Lufthansa will face irreparable damage because Ryanair is slagging it off.'

'It's typical of Lufthansa to run into court at the first possible opportunity. They creep into courts late at night without telling anybody and they get injunctions that are designed to prevent German consumers being made aware of competition in air travel. The public affairs department of the courts never told us the case was coming up.'

'The only thing that Lufthansa have not yet got is an injunction on from the German courts to prevent Ryanair calling itself Ryanair.'

'This is just chapter two of anti-competitive behaviour by airlines. First we had Aer Lingus, then BA and now we have Lufthansa.'

'Through all these court cases, Lufthansa has probably created more publicity for us than we've had on any other route we've launched. We are now one of the best-known brands in Germany thanks to Lufthansa suing us in every court in Germany.'

'There's a lot of nonsense being talked about Eastern Europe with the expansion of the EU and so on, but I want to carry rich Germans to France and Spain and Italy.'

'Ryanair's immediate success in Germany highlights yet again the consumer behaviour law already established by

Wal-Mart namely, that customers will flock to out-of-town secondary locations in order to avail of lower prices and avoid congestion. Many of the so-called experts, most of whom seem to work for Lufthansa, who predicted that Ryanair's low fares would not take off in Germany, appear to have ignored the tremendous success of low-price retailers such as Aldi, Lidl, McDonald's and IKEA in the German market.'

'Sometimes there is not even a road to the airports we fly to. It is immaterial. Passengers will find their way to the airport if the air fares are low enough. Dr Jürgen Weber, the chief executive of Lufthansa, spent the last two years attending conferences all over Germany swearing that Ryanair would not work in Germany and that Frankfurt-Hahn Airport would not work because the passengers would not go there. Two years later, passengers get there because they are saving €400 over the average fare charged by Lufthansa.'

On concerns from German airports operator Fraport that passengers would not fly from Hahn: 'That's bullshit. People will go there just because airfares are cheap.'

'Germans will crawl bollock-naked over broken glass to get low fares.'

SOUTHWEST AIRLINES

'Herb Kelleher is like God.'

'We went to look at Southwest Airlines in the US. It was like the road to Damascus. This was the way to make Ryanair work. I met with Herb Kelleher. I passed out about midnight, and when I woke up again at about 3 a.m. Kelleher was still there, the bastard, pouring himself another bourbon and smoking. I thought I'd pick his brains and come away with the Holy Grail. The next day I couldn't remember a thing.'

'Southwest was a big guiding thing for me. Before I heard about Southwest I had seen two airlines in Ireland, Ryanair and Aer Lingus, both of which were blindingly incompetent. They had complicated check-in, business class, travel agent that, all the rest of that crap, and were turning planes around in an hour. Then you went to Southwest, banging aircraft out after 15 minutes. They were phenomenal; passengers loved it. You could just see efficiency. I saw it with my own eyes and said, "We can do this in Europe."'

'All we've done is copy Herb Kelleher's successful model. In fact, we're maybe the only people to copy it successfully and maybe take it beyond where Southwest has gone with it. But other than that it's still Southwest's model.'

'Originally Southwest didn't charge for drinks on board and now they do, because of us.'

'We decided to follow the kind of low-fares formula that Southwest Airlines has pioneered in the US. It seemed blindingly obvious that if we couldn't out-service Aer Lingus with better business class and better service, we could certainly offer better fares.'

'We like to think in Ryanair we have a number of traits in common with Southwest. Firstly it's run by the drunken Irish, and we like to pride ourselves on our ability to party, and fly while over the limit. Secondly the Irish and Texans have a number of other things in common, like humility, religion and gun laws.'

'Southwest has had periods in its history where profits have taken a dip for a period of time, or the share price has taken a dip for a time, but it's still the mother and father of low-fares airlines.'

'If I were Southwest, I wouldn't be worried. Southwest is the equivalent of Wal-Mart. No one can outdo Wal-Mart. They have the pricing power. It's not a temporary phenomenon. We're competing in a market where most of our competitors are trying to charge prices of Bergdorfs or Saks. Air transport is just a commodity.'

'Over the next five to ten years we will see the emergence of three to four large price-gouging carriers and one very large low-fares airline. There can only be one lowest-cost airline, there can't be two. There is only one really powerful low-fares airline in Europe and it is called Ryanair. And there is only one in the United States and it is called Southwest Airlines. This is not a great business to be in if you are somebody else.'

'"No formula lasts forever." That is true but as Southwest Airlines (32 years), McDonald's (almost 50 years) and Wal-Mart (over 40 years) indicate, if you continue to provide an efficient service at lowest prices, then you can continue to grow a business strongly for many years.'

'Once we saw what Southwest was doing we thought this could be the way forward: selling at the lowest possible price to the maximum number of people. As Southwest has repeatedly demonstrated in the US for many years, the lowest-cost carrier always wins.'

'How important is Herb Kelleher? The man is a genius.'

EASYJET

'easyJet are not the brightest sandwiches in the picnic basket.'

On the founder of easyJet: 'There are very few examples of where I would follow Stelios in anything. He's Greek and I'm Irish. The Greeks will never outdo the Irish in anything. We'll even outdo them in drinking. He's the son of a billionaire. He could have been a rich tosser but at least he did something and set up an airline.'

'Ryanair was the first low-fares/no-frills airline in Europe, and the first low-fares/no-frills route was flying from the UK seven years before easyJet started. Ryanair also began flying between London and Glasgow before easyJet even started flying its first route. Whatever Stelios and easyJet may have done, they certainly weren't the first or the founders—Ryanair was.'

On the founder of easyJet: 'Those of us who sell the lowest air fares just get on with it, and those who do not write whingeing letters to newspapers.'

When easyJet bought the British Airways subsidiary Go: 'Embarking on an acquisition of another higher-fare airline at this time is certainly a ballsy move. I will be taking lessons in humility now that we are, for the time being, Europe's second-largest low-fares airline.'

'When we were a much smaller company, we compared ourselves to British Airways. But they are such a mess, most people just feel sorry for them. Now we're turning the guns on easyJet.'

'Our message to easyJet is simple. You can't match Ryanair's low fares and you can't match Ryanair's punctuality and customer service either. There is no need to wait for easyJet's high fares and crap punctuality. While easyJet hibernates this winter, millions of Ryanair passengers will be enjoying Europe's lowest fares, best punctuality and customer service.'

'We want to eliminate the idea that easyJet is somehow a low-cost carrier. It isn't. Its average fares are 70% higher than ours. It's time to sort out who is the low-fare airline. It is Ryanair. It is not easyJet. They are a medium-fare airline.'

When sitting and wearing army combat fatigues on a WWII tank outside easyJet's headquarters at Luton Airport: 'I've been told and it's no lie, easyJet's fares are way too high. It's about peace, not war. We want a piece of British Airways, a piece of Lufthansa and a piece of easyJet. We are liberating the public from easyJet's high fares.'

'easyJet is fundamentally a good operation, except that's it's not a low-fares operation. But it's still very competitive with British Airways, Air France and Lufthansa, and I think they'll do very well.'

'There's scope for easyJet to be a profitable airline competing with the numbnuts in Europe as long as they stay out of our way. easyJet are a convenient target for us to have a go at, but they do what they do, and we do what we do, but we do it that much better.'

On news that easyJet was to launch new services between London Gatwick and Cork, Knock and Shannon, and breaking into song: 'Suicide is painless… and easyJet is aimless. If they really want to compete with us why don't they lower their fares and come to Dublin?'

'The future is not about the competition between Ryanair and easyJet because, with the greatest respect, that competition is over. Eventually you will lose to Ryanair because we have a lower cost base. They are British Midland Mark II.'

OTHER AIRLINES

'They're all screwed. Doomed.'

'We are launching our latest price war across Europe to go and kick competitors when we can. The best reason to get out of bed is to beat the pulp out of your competition and they want to beat the pulp out of us.'

'There is a lot of stupid competition out there losing money. We are not reducing our low fares because we are a charity. There is some below-cost selling, easyJet, British Airways, everyone is at it. It's part of a land grab going on in Europe and we will always be lower than anyone else.'

'As far as the competition is concerned, we will never join them, but we will keep beating them.'

'Full-service airlines are basket cases. They're incredibly high-cost, very inefficient, and they're locked into businesses where yields are in inexorable decline. These are stupid businesses for the amount of capital tied up in them. They never make any money. The sooner they go to the wall the better.'

'Code-sharing, alliances, and connections are all about "how do we screw the poor customer for more money?"'

'If you put two expensive, loss-making airlines together, then you just get another even more expensive and even greater loss-making airline.'

'There are going to be three big players: the BA family, which will be BA and Iberia; Air France with KLM; and probably Alitalia and Lufthansa with SAS and Austrian. Those three will be the carriers for connecting flights across Europe. If you are flying long-haul you will fly with one of them and be pushed through Heathrow, Charles de Gaulle or Frankfurt. What the big guys are going to do is keep raising fares across the hub airports because they can and they will drive people through those hubs. We're going after the big guys, because that's where the easiest competition is.'

'There are the three high-fares rapists—British Airways, Lufthansa and Air France.'

'We would like to apologise to ordinary French consumers and visitors who will continue to be forced to pay Air France's rip-off high fares of nearly €800 for Strasbourg-to-London flights instead of the €9 (plus taxes) one-way fares charged by Ryanair.'

On being delayed at a Paris airport because his Air France flight had been overbooked: 'I was about to give them the "Do you know who I am?" thing, but thought that would have had me bumped out of the airport, never mind the flight. Fortunately there was a second flight, or I'd have had to beg to get on an easyJet flight.'

'Sabena is a bankrupt company. Let it go bankrupt. It deserves to be bankrupt.'

'Alitalia? I would not want it if it were given to me as a present. Alitalia could have a future, but only if it is free from political influence and union pressures.'

'Competition from other low-cost carriers is just not an issue. We compete with British Airways, Alitalia, Lufthansa, sas on routes all over Continental Europe. Why the hell would we fear Go? Its lost £21 million on a £41-million turnover. And Virgin Express is a tiny airline which has issued 12 profit warnings in the last four quarters. It's not an airline that anybody in Europe would fear or acknowledge as a serious threat.'

On competing with Richard Branson's Virgin Express: 'I thought, ok, Dickie, let's have you.'

'If you look at the low-fares industry, Kelleher is still heads and shoulders above everybody else. And you can count the rest of the successes on the fingers of one hand. Branson, who's clearly a genius at making money, got burned in the low-fares industry. Virgin Express was a dog, it sold out to sn Brussels. And he's done clearly very well with his other businesses; he's a multibillionaire. Branson is a genius for getting half a billion quid out of the Singaporeans for 49% of his business.'

'There is going to be the mother and father of all fare wars. There is going to be a ferocious bloodbath. The only airlines that are going to survive this are the ones that are making money now. Of the low-cost airlines, that means us and easyJet.'

'Three airlines in the States have gone bankrupt in the last month. Alitalia is teetering on the edge of bank- ruptcy. Clickair is losing so much money they don't know what to do. Sky Europe will probably go bust. Wizz Air, it's harder to say. As for Vueling, I wouldn't take it if you made a present of it to me. If Vueling was losing money with oil at $65 a barrel then it's bankrupt at $95. Air Berlin is lost. We'll be very happy to see them all go bust.'

'Personally, I wouldn't buy an Air Berlin ticket this winter.'

On the planned launch of Now Airlines, a Luton-based competing low-fares airline: 'Never.'

'We must continue to grow organically and not get into the business of buying other airlines, setting up subsidiaries or getting involved in other businesses.'

On buying Buzz for £15m: 'While it has been our policy to avoid acquisitions, this opportunity, at this nominal cost, is the type of offer which we could not refuse. It was petty cash, a bargain.'

'Buzz had 20 French destinations; we were going to cut that down to about 10. We would have an auction and get cost deals out of them. Buzz had loads of routes they were flying twice a week and three times a week and we were going daily. We had bigger aircraft, lower cost base; we knew what we were at. We make no bones about playing the airports off against each other. The airports that lost could fuck off.'

'Buzz got saddled by KLM with the shittiest set of aircraft in the fleet, flying to shitty airports and with a few too many employees for an airline carrying two million passengers. There will be hell, brim fire and damnation. Let there be no misunderstanding about this. If BALPA or any of the others want to go on strike, it won't be a question of sacking pilots, we'll close down Buzz.'

'The unions at Buzz would have played ducks and drakes with us if we were trying desperately to keep the airline going. We said "Fuck that, we're going to shut it for a month." The unions realised "Shit, this is serious." And shutting it down was the master stroke because then we weren't dealing with any of the bullshit.'

To Buzz workers: 'There's no point in sugaring pills. This is losing shedloads of money and has to be turned round. We're not going to sit around having consultations or going through some laborious process. This is not stopping for anybody. For those who don't want to sign up to the project, the door's out there on the left.'

On repainting Buzz aircraft: 'That strikes us a waste of money. We will simply scratch out the Buzz name and scratch in Ryanair.'

On returning Buzz planes to KLM: 'We'll fly to Schiphol, load the keys in through the window and run.'

'Imitation is the best form of flattery.'

On the prospect of a merger with another airline: 'No thanks, I'd rather have a social disease.'

On offering advice to other airlines' bosses: 'They can fuck off and do their own work.'

IRELAND

'We are God's own children.'

'The airline industry is full of bullshitters, liars and drunks and we excel at all three in Ireland. We will be the world's biggest airline.'

'They don't call us the fighting Irish for nothing. We have been the travel innovators of Europe. We built the roads and laid the rails. Now it's the airlines.'

'I'm Irish and we don't have to prove anything. We bow to nobody.'

'There is no shortage of ambition here. We'll stuff every one of them in Europe, we won't be second or third and saying, "Didn't we do well?" Ryanair shows what Irish people can achieve when we put our minds to it. We don't limit ourselves to being just good in Ireland. Let's take on the world.'

'You can look at us as a small Irish company stuffing it to British Airways and Lufthansa and Air France. This is not work for me. This is sheer fun at this stage. I'll have at least another 10 years here, antagonising and annoying other high-fares airlines around Europe, and probably everyone else as well. I'm convinced that nothing will stop us unless we screw it up ourselves.'

'The next 12 months will be a catastrophe for tourism. The traffic has collapsed from the UK. It's stagnating at 0%; given that sterling is at 76p we should be getting invaded. For the first time in 16 years, numbers could actually decline next year. Tourism in this country next year is fucked. The tourism industry is facing job losses of up to 30,000, which will make the dot-com burst look like a tea party.'

'Tourism Ireland are a complete waste of time. They talk a lot and don't do much and believe that if they come up with a small amount of money, this is a huge concession by them. Thankfully, our growth and our success isn't going to be dependent on Tourism Ireland. If it was, we would be dead. Tourism Ireland has talked a very good story, but the delivery has been poor.'

'I think we can revolutionise Irish tourism to and from Europe, and I think it is a cause worth fighting for. We believe the way of fixing tourism in this country is low-cost access. Ireland is expensive to get to but we are changing that. The only ones I hear talking about Ireland being expensive are RTÉ journalists. This country is not too expensive for the Germans, the French and the Italians. It's too expensive because it costs £600 to get here. And who does the blame lie with? Stupid, incompetent ministers.'

'In many respects, we created the Irish tourism boom that took place between 1985 and 1995. The dogs in the street know what our contribution to tourism is. There's many more UK tourists coming in now because it's a low-

cost destination. Dublin–London is now the busiest international route in Europe. People do this bullshit
analysis: why has Dublin boomed? Was it Temple Bar,
U2 or the sunny Irish personality? Bullshit, we made
London–Dublin cheap.'

'The key thing here is access. I have no doubt about the
ability of the tourism industry in this country to respond.
There is an awful lot of nonsense talked or revisionism
going on about the 1980s. Which came first in Irish
tourism? Did the tourists all start coming here in the mid-
1980s because we had Guinness, nice personalities, were
grand crack and it was a grand place for a stag party and
all the rest of it? This place was like Albania in 1985.'

'I am trying to convey what Ryanair is out doing at a time
when Irish tourism is in the toilet, there is world recession, war in Iraq and a feeling of doom and gloom.'

'On the issue of low-cost passengers into a high cost
country, there is an awful lot of old nonsense talked in
Ireland about it being high-cost. Yes, it is not cheap. We
are no longer Albania or Poland.'

'We can do this again from Europe, so that instead of just
getting stag parties from Leeds, Bradford, Sheffield or
Bristol, we will bring in people from France, Spain and
Italy. They are dying to come to Ireland. I have a pain in
my ear going around to all these airports saying we will
fly to them from London, Frankfurt, Milan and so on.
They say, "We would really love, Monsieur, a route to
Dublin or Shannon." We must reply, "Sorry, the Irish
Government won't allow us." They are mystified until we
explain afterwards the subtlety that the Irish Government, through its airports, wants to screw us for every
passenger we bring here.'

On CIÉ: 'In fairness, you couldn't get any worse than CIÉ. What sort of company highlights the fact that they're crap? We'll wipe the floor with them. They have a rubbish service, and they won't be able to compete with us. If I were them I'd be quaking in my boots right now. Whatever they decide to charge for their Dublin–Cork rail service, we will undercut it. There is no doubt there are huge changes coming given the new rolling stock on the railroad and the improvements to the Dublin–Cork road. I think trains certainly pose the greatest challenge to Cork Airport. The CIÉ service would be all right if, like the airlines, you could book on and be guaranteed a seat. The idea, particularly at weekends, of standing for two hours and kids jumping around and queues for the toilets and all the rest of it—that's not a service. That's the way cattle travel. I think we're going to clear up the business traffic. The only way to get a guaranteed seat by train to Cork is to pay through the nose for a first-class ticket. People say that there isn't a culture of internal flying in this country because it's such a small place, but there is an appreciation for lower prices and that's why our planes between Dublin and Cork will be full all the time. Irish Rail won't be able to compete. Let's say they lower their price to €10—we'll offer it to the consumer for €9.'

'Internal flights in Ireland are a joke. This Dáil committee should investigate the amount of subsidies that are being lashed out by the Department of Transport under the Public Service Obligation for internal routes. The extent of these subsidies is a scandal when there are many other things that could be done with €25 million, such as in the health service. I am not sure giving it to rich business-people getting their early morning flights out of regional airports is a good use of that money, but it is not the business I am in. This year the total for about 250,000 passengers will be about €24 million. The average subsidy is €100 each—that is what we as taxpayers are paying the few people who do fly between these places in the west of Ireland. Aer Arann and the other crowd up in Donegal are getting €100 for every passenger who flies with them. Our average fare on 125 routes across Europe is €43, yet the Government is subsidising these companies. It would be cheaper to write them all a cheque for €50 and tell them to get the train or bus, which would probably reduce the subvention to CIÉ. Nestors run a fantastic service from Galway Airport to Dublin Airport for about €15. In that way the Government could save €85 of this bloody subsidy, which is a joke. There is no huge demand for the service. Given the improvements to national motorways and the increased frequency of rail services to the regions, these subsidies are unjustified and totally unnecessary. This money could be better spent on our healthcare service or education system. Just think how many additional school classrooms, Special Needs Assistants or how many hospital beds could be funded by this €45m.'

On Ryanair tendering for and winning a Public Service Obligation route from Dublin to Kerry: 'If unjustified subsidies are available, then Ryanair is right to apply for and win them.'

On the Consumers' Association of Ireland: 'In order to emphasise Ryanair's refusal to levy fuel surcharges, our guarantee of lowest fares and to show that the Consumers' Association of Ireland is talking rubbish as usual, when bleating on about non-existent hidden charges (which are most definitely not "hidden" and are discretionary/avoidable), Ryanair today released 300,000 free seats (that is no taxes, no fees and no charges, for the idiots in the CAI) for travel on selected flights on Mondays to Thursdays in June. Perhaps the misguided CAI would now address the real rip-off of consumers, which comprises non-discretionary fuel surcharges and ever-increasing costs being fleeced from passengers at Dublin Airport, where parking charges again rose recently by 50% without even a murmur from the Government-funded CAI.'

'Concerning the threat of moving the Ryanair head-quarters from Dublin: there is no possibility of that whatsoever. I should say, however, that the Ryanair head-quarters are not in Dublin, they are in Mullingar, which is obviously the centre of the universe.'

'This is an Irish company and we are very proud of that fact. It is not moving anywhere else. It is one of the great Irish success stories. We would lose an awful lot of the culture and the 'can-do' attitude if we were ever to move it away from Dublin. I also wish to endorse the tax policies of the present Government, whereby corporation tax is down at around 12.5%, which has a significant bearing on our allegiance to Ireland for the location of our head-quarters. Mercifully this is not Russia.'

'We don't look upon ourselves as an Irish airline any more. We look upon ourselves as a European airline.'

'Ryanair is effectively based in the UK.'

'It would be inconceivable that anyone would treat Ryanair as not Irish, otherwise we'd be homeless, or state-less. We're an Irish-owned, -operated and -headquartered airline.'

'If we were an American computer company offering 4,000 jobs, the Irish Government would build statues to honour us, name buildings after us and ask what they can do for us to attract us to Ireland. However, because we are Irish, the Government does not seem to want to follow our plan.'

'I am entitled to get a lot of criticism. I am opinionated, I am certainly not shy about holding forth on my opinions but regardless of whether I am being criticised, people in Ryanair are doing such an outstanding job. They get far too little credit in Ireland for what is by far and away and if not the most successful Irish business in the last 20 years.'

'The extent of the ignorance of what Ryanair does here is breathtaking. Few people seem to realise how big we are, how successful we are across Europe and the fact that this is the only country in Europe where what we do is not welcomed with open arms or encouraged.'

'We are running probably one of the most successful new company stories of the 1980s and 1990s here, yet, amazingly, this is the only country in which we are continuously blocked from replicating this success for the good of consumers and visitors to this country and for tourism.'

'Maybe it's just an Irish thing. We have spent our life having the shit kicked out of us. I'm a small Paddy over here in Europe trying to punch above his weight in terms of making noise. As Richard Branson demonstrated, the way to punch above your weight is to shout your mouth off.'

'Hey, they don't like us in Ireland, I don't care. We're not running for election.'

AER RIANTA

'Aer Rianta got the figures wrong, not for the first time.'

'The facilities at Dublin Airport are inadequate, over-crowded and ludicrously expensive. They are a testament to the failure of the Aer Rianta monopoly. The Irish taxpayer, through Aer Rianta, is investing heavily in hotels and airports in Birmingham and Dusseldorf, yet we are subjected to Third World facilities at this nation's principal airport.'

'Dublin Airport is ridiculously expensive. What you want is low-cost facilities, not gold-plated mausoleums. Where in the legislation does it say Aer Rianta can subsidise the fat cats waddling down to Pier C to board their British Midland morning business flights to Heathrow?'

'Aer Rianta spent £50 million on a five-storey extension which nobody wants to use. The new baggage hall is something designed by Russian architects. Pier C was designed by Aer Rianta to win an architectural competition rather than serve the needs of airlines.'

'What goes on at Dublin Airport on a daily basis is a scandal. Aer Rianta freely builds in the red zones. It blocks everybody else from doing so. The Kennel Club was built in a red zone, as was a leisure complex.'

'Aer Rianta got 13 expressions of interest but about 11 consisted of a three line-letter stating, "We hereby express an interest in building a new terminal at Dublin Airport."'

'If we offer to build the terminal for nothing the investment is zero. There is no possibility of costs rising at Dublin Airport as a result of some moron from Mullingar offering to build a terminal for free for the Government. It is inconceivable that Aer Rianta's costs would increase as a result of somebody else building a terminal free for it. It is wrong. It has never happened in the history of competition, since Adam Smith wrote "The Wealth of Nations" in 1778. Competition reduces costs and prices.'

'The chairman of Aer Rianta announced that it wanted to build an internal railway system at Dublin Airport. They cannot run an airport but now he believes they can run a train system out there. That would cost €100 million. There is no requirement for it. Nobody needs it or wants it.'

'Aer Rianta supports the building of a rail line from Dublin Airport to the centre of Dublin. No one asked the airlines or the customers if they needed it. The cost, I understand, has gone from €2.5 billion to €4 billion. This is an airport that already has 14 million passengers a year. Somehow, unbelievably, 14 million passengers a year manage to make it in and out between Dublin Airport and the centre of Dublin. I know it is difficult at times because the M1 motorway is being extended, but we do not need to spend €4 billion building something for the next two or three million passengers that come to Dublin Airport. Can Aer Rianta be run better? Yes, absolutely.'

'Dublin has 14 million passengers a year. One runway can handle about 30 million passengers a year. Gatwick this year has one runway and will deal with 36 million passengers. This, again, is Aer Rianta trying to spend another €200 million to €500 million a year, from which it can then recover income. None of the airlines wants a second runway at Dublin Airport; it should not be built and the regulator is not allowing it to be built. Nevertheless, Aer Rianta is still pushing ahead with the scheme. It is complete lunacy. The Government should tell Aer Rianta to stop.'

'Part of the problem is that there is a regulatory regime in Aer Rianta whereby the company's income is capped at a percentage of its total capital base. The whole purpose or *raison d'être* of Aer Rianta is to spend as much capital as is humanly possible because the more it spends, or the more money it wastes on building infrastructure, the higher its income cap will be for the next couple of years. This is why there are all these crazy ideas.'

'A construction company got planning permission about two years ago to build a competing car park at the end of the runway at Dublin Airport. Despite repeated objections from Aer Rianta, the Irish Aviation Authority approved of it in terms of safety as it did not interfere with the runways. Aer Rianta has spent two years pursuing a legal challenge to prevent a competitive car park being built in Dublin Airport. Meanwhile, the daily rate for car parking was jacked up from €12 to €30 by Aer Rianta.'

'The big problem at the airport is the high cost of car parking. Charging €30 a day to park a car in a field Aer Rianta got for free from the Government three years ago is an obscenity. It is another monopoly rip-off. However, under our plans, which would not cost Aer Rianta or the Government a penny, we would build two more multi-storey car parks. Part of the proposal is that we would guarantee that the daily rate of car parking would be €10, half the current cost. Can we make money on that? I do not know, but we will do it anyway.'

'We have no success on costs in Dublin or in Stansted, but at the other 140-odd airports we fly to, there has been almost universal reductions in not just airport costs but handling costs as well. We moved seven planes out of Stansted last winter; I think that number will rise and the process will start at Dublin. There's only one way to deal with a monopoly like this and that is to reduce traffic.'

'I do not give a hoot what other airlines say to Aer Rianta. I run my business. Aer Rianta should be running its business. What do we get from Aer Rianta? The back of the hand.'

'Aer Rianta trots out all this stuff about whether it is accepted that there is a cost for the passenger and that the airport has a cost for this, that and the other. I do not accept any of that. Aer Lingus used to come up with the same old trot back in the late 1980s. It said that the average fare to London was £150, that this was cheap by international standards and everyone knew there was a cost for flying people to London. Miraculously, 15 years later the average cost has fallen by the guts of two-thirds. I get a pain in my ear listening to the people in the media in this country trotting on all the time about how everything has gone up since the euro. Nobody bloody mentions the air fares. They are still going down.'

'We would provide internal flights between Shannon, Dublin and Cork, but we will not pay Aer Rianta €10 a passenger in Dublin, €10 a passenger in Cork and €10 a passenger in Shannon. If it wants to provide the runways and tell us we can fly for free, we will happily run those routes.'

'Seán Barrett, a leading transport economist, has made the point that airports are pretty much like shopping centres. Shopping centres will do a deal with Dunnes Stores or Marks and Spencer to be the anchor tenant because they will hoover in lots of people. Then the centres get higher charges from all the other tenants. Why does Aer Rianta not act on a similar basis?'

'We have 40 new airports all over Europe ready and waiting for us to launch new routes. We have nine other bases ready. Aer Rianta says they will not cut us a deal here. Fine, we have plenty of alternatives, but we would like to do it in this country. They then ask why we want to do it in this country—is it because we want to make a bundle of money here? Yes, of course we do, but I can make a bundle of money elsewhere.'

'Aer Rianta will tell you that Ireland is losing passengers because of the Gulf War, the loss of duty-free or whatever—anything other than admit that it is their fault.'

'It is no surprise that after 10 successive years of record growth, Ireland's tourism has shuddered to a halt. There is no point in expecting a monopoly to encourage competition.'

'The thought of our airport monopoly, Aer Rianta, making a complaint to the Competition Authority fills me with joy and wonder.'

'You want to take on monopolies, you've got to be ready to fight. The fights are good for the soul.'

On sending a Ryanair cabin crew charity calendar to the

Irish Airport Regulator: 'This will give you something interesting and uplifting to hang over your desk, and to look at, as you and your twenty colleagues while away the many idle hours between now and the next Airport Charges Review.'

'Is it possible for the company to be run better? Where do I start? Let me give an example. Aer Rianta is the Iraq of Irish tourism. It is an inefficient dictatorship.'

On claims that he impersonated an Evening Herald journalist when telephoning Aer Rianta's press office: 'No, I think that whatever they're smoking they should give it up. I ring Aer Rianta about six times a day, I'm not commenting on that. No, I'm not saying whether I did ring or not.'

On how best to settle his differences with Aer Rianta: 'With Semtex, preferably during a board meeting. Sack the board! Aer Rianta is a monument to incompetence and stupidity.'

DUBLIN AIRPORT

'Dublin Airport has descended into a farce.'

'Anybody who's come through Dublin Airport over the last five years would know it's bloody disastrous and it needs to be broken up. In the Dublin Airport Authority you have the masters of waste, inefficiency and incompetence. The Dublin Airport Authority which is responsible for this Third World facility is to be rewarded for its incompetence.'

'Even by the standards of the Dublin Aviation Authority and the Department of Transport a 100% cost over-run before they have even applied for planning permission sets a new high hurdle for incompetence and Government waste.'

'Competition is a very healthy thing and Dublin Airport needs a lot more of it. It's a fucking monopoly gone mad. Unless you have more competition, you are going to have more of this crap. It seemed to have been designed by Russians.'

'You can't trust the Dublin Airport Authority to build an efficient, low-cost terminal. It is badly designed, in the wrong location, and is five times more expensive than other similar terminal facilities in the UK or Europe.'

'The Dublin Airport Authority couldn't organise a piss-up in a brewery.'

On expected chaos caused by many new Ryanair routes at Dublin Airport: 'It's not my problem.'

'If someone as bright as Dermot Desmond thinks it's the right time to sell London City Airport, surely you would think that the halfwits in the Irish Government would think maybe it's the right time to offload the stakes in Birmingham and Dusseldorf Airports. Neither of them makes any contribution to Irish tourism or the Irish economy generally.'

'Dublin Airport is looking for an increase in the passenger fees from €6.50 to €9.50. The regulator has come back and said, "No, we'll only give you €7.75." So Dublin Airport will come up to him and say, "We're very unhappy with this," you know, but they still got a 25% price increase.'

'The big problem in terms of access from Dublin Airport to the city is the airport roundabout. Mercifully that is about to be solved by taking the M1 directly north, which will split the traffic from Swords, thus eliminating that bottleneck. Most of those who travel from the west, from where all the best people come, to access the airport travel by the Navan road and the M50.'

'The Aircoach service does a terrific job in taking people across the city to numerous destinations. Deregulation of the bus operations to and from Dublin Airport has revolutionised access. Dublin Airport is not a big airport. Even our plans see passenger numbers rising from 14 million to 20 million a year. It is not the biggest airport in the world at 20 million passengers a year, so please do not waste €4 billion building a railway system to the airport. A railway system may be needed to Swords and other new towns and if it runs past the airport, Godspeed.'

'It is crazy to put in a rail system, especially if it costs €4 billion. Where would it take people? Would it take them to Ballsbridge? In Ballsbridge they can pay for taxis, buses or whatever.'

'The €1.5-billion Dublin Metro is the latest vanity project for the Department of Transport.'

On a radar failure at Dublin Airport: 'We're still not getting answers either from the Irish Aviation Authority who, of course, as usual in a crisis, disappear down a drain, or the Department of Transport, the people who couldn't manage any part of Ireland's transport infrastructure. They all go into hiding because none of them has to deal with real human beings.'

'We, as the largest airline in the country, have not been consulted on either the location, the cost or designing of this terminal at Dublin Airport. It's an absolute bloody disgrace that's its not going to be here until late 2009 and how you can spend €1.2 billion when the private sector offered to build it for €200 million is equally a disgrace. It's a shambles.'

'We do not need a small temporary tent at Dublin Airport for this summer. We need to push on and get the second terminal built.'

'What solution have I for Dublin Airport? Let us build a second terminal. If you do not like Ryanair, let someone build a second one, but please do not waste another five years, which is what the wise men's committee said it would take. We could have it built within 18 months. There is a site and we have offered to pay for it. We will design, develop and build the terminal. What the hell is going to take five years? The first 10 months of this are planning, consideration and consultation. We are so busy bloody consulting, nobody bothers doing anything.'

On online check-in: 'The introduction of this new technology simplifies the lives of the security staff. Only in Dublin Airport, where you have the trade unions with a lock on it, are they looking obviously to go to the Labour Relations Court, looking for more money for doing less work. The Dublin Airport Authority had no problem with it, for the same reasons we don't. It reduces queues and it makes the work of the security staff even simpler. It's not up to a bunch of trade union headbangers to decide who will and who won't go through the airport. Any time you try to introduce something to ease passengers' journeys, you have unions saying we need to go to the Labour Relations Court.'

'Unless there's some incentive for us to move to the basement of the Black Hole of Calcutta, we'll stay where we are. Passengers are just shovelled into a hole.'

'Fine Gael's second Dublin airport idea is insane and stupid.'

'The only two cities that British Airways did not fly to in 1985 were Tirana in Albania and Dublin. It was expensive to get to and nobody wanted to bloody come here. Jim Mitchell at the time and subsequent ministers revolutionised it by introducing, partly by accident, competition to Aer Lingus. Access costs came down. No longer did people have to come here on bloody boats.'

'Dublin Airport could easily operate and not charge the airlines and still be profitable. One can argue that it would be more profitable than at present if it was run properly.'

'When it comes to car parking, in Dublin Airport some of the car parks are closer to Co. Kildare than they are the airport itself.'

On Dublin Airport car-parking prices: 'Brinks-Allied Security weren't the only people robbed this week.'

SHANNON AIRPORT

'Shannon is dead in the winter.'

'With Irish tourism in the toilet, a worldwide recession, a war in Iraq and people not flying across the Atlantic, Shannon wants to increase costs for the only low-fares airline which is growing traffic to and from Shannon. This is the behaviour and mentality of a monopoly.'

'Forget the US. The transatlantic stopover is gone and the sooner Shannon gets over it and gets on with life, the better. The future for Shannon Airport is as a gateway for tourism into the west. We should forget the Americans: they are gone. This airport is looking down the barrel of losing the transatlantic stopover. That is going, no matter how it tries to keep it.'

'Aer Rianta have spent £30 million on a terminal in Shannon and no one is coming to it. Meanwhile, you cannot build a dog box in Dublin. They have to do something about Shannon because in two years' time, when the Americans are overflying it, it will be a goner.'

'The fact that Royal Jordanian will now be stopping off with 100,000 people for wee-wees in Shannon will really guarantee the future of the airport and tourism in the mid-western region. Who knows, it might even create one or two jobs for lavatory cleaners in the area. If the truth hurts them that's their problem. They do nothing for the local economy, but this has nothing to do with Royal Jordanian. Last year it was Pakistan International stopping off for fuel and piss stops. This is between Ryanair and Mary O'Rourke. If Royal Jordanian is hurt, such is life. If they want to open up a route, we'll apologise.'

'Aer Lingus's transatlantic flights will be gone from Shannon by next September. Take it as read. I have absolutely no doubt in my mind and I have no insight. But my view is that Aer Lingus transferring Shannon-Heathrow to Belfast is a precursor for Aer Lingus to transfer the transatlantic flights up there as well.'

'As regards the five-year deal at Cork, that is the problem with Aer Rianta, it is a public relations stunt. They dressed up a five-year deal at Cork Airport—it is free in year one, there is an 80% discount in year two, and 60% in year three. This is a five-year deal of rising costs, yet they want us to come up with low-fare services and grow traffic. I will be happily gone from Ryanair before most of these deals unwind.'

'Shannon, or Ireland, was about to lose the Frankfurt route because instead of sending the aircraft from Frankfurt to Shannon, we were going to send it to somewhere else in Europe where costs would have been less than one-fifth of what Aer Rianta was charging at Shannon. As luck would have it, the Kerrymen, who are not shy about coming forward, called us on the Tuesday before we were to announce the pull-out on the Thursday to say we could fly to Kerry for a great deal less than Shannon was charging. Kerry now has the route from Frankfurt. If Shannon take the same stance on those routes as they did with Hahn, then we'll drop them. People don't care if you fly them into Knock, Kerry or Shannon, they just want to visit the region at the lowest cost. We are being charged less in Kerry Airport, and that is on the record. I will not say by how much because the cute Kerry boys do not want me to tell.'

'We have advocated that Shannon be freed from the dead hand of Aer Rianta and be allowed to do deals with Ryanair on low cost terms. Shannon wanted to go from charges of nil to €6 a skull.'

'On the question of management at Shannon, to be manager of Shannon and Cork Airports must be the two most difficult jobs in the country because they are told what to do by the guys in Dublin. They cannot do anything without getting it cleared through Dublin. In the good old days when Liam Skelly used to run Shannon and Barry Roche ran Cork, they were run as independent republics. They used not tell Dublin what was going on. Those were the good old days.'

'I was asked if I would recommend management change at Shannon Airport. Without wishing to use my Iraq simile, I would not. I think the management at Shannon Airport are fine. What Aer Rianta needs, however, is regime change—in other words, get the bloody regime in Baghdad—sorry, Dublin Airport—out of there and allow Shannon to work in the interests of Shannon, and give the guys running Cork Airport the freedom to develop traffic there in the interests of Cork.'

'Our relationships with Cork Airport are excellent. I would go on record and say that the management of Cork and Shannon Airports are absolutely fantastic, committed, very able and bright people, but doing so would probably doom their careers forever with the Aer Rianta organisation were we to compliment them. So, I think we should just include them and say we do not like them either.'

'I hold no grudge against the people who run Shannon or Cork Airports. They do a good job but their hands are tied behind their backs because they are told what to do all the time by the "Saddam Husseins" in Dublin. They have no possibility of running those airports in the interests of their communities, as they should be allowed do. I know some terms to describe that but they might not be parliamentary.'

'I would take responsibility for Cork and Shannon Airports from Aer Rianta. I would ensure they were free starting off and would give management responsibility to whatever local structure was in place, be it SFADCO or some other publicly owned bodies in Cork, either Bord Fáilte, the new Irish Tourism Board, or whatever. I would challenge that management every year by saying they will get the sack if they do not increase the traffic at Shannon or Cork Airports this year by 20%, and if they increased by 20% I would give them a €100,000 bonus. I would have only one meeting with them a year. That is all that has to be done.'

'In this country, we should get out of the notion that Ireland is a wonderful destination or that any places in Ireland are wonderful for some unique reason—they are not. If it is low-cost we will get hundreds of thousands of people to go there. That is not to say that Shannon is a bad destination; it is not. I think Shannon has fantastic potential as a gateway to the west. Equally, however, as you get lost trying to find Frankfurt-Hahn Airport in the middle of Germany, so do lots of tourists get lost trying to find Shannon Airport, as I do sometimes on my way through Limerick.'

'Shannon has an incredible future as the gateway to the west. The argument can be made that in Dublin we have enough tourists, although we need a few more. The roads have been improved, the M1 motorway will be built and it will be fairly easy to get in and out of Dublin. The great feature of European tourists is that most of them do not want to go to Temple Bar; they want to go to the west. That is the draw for the Germans, Italians and French. The Government is working to address regional imbalance through the spatial strategy. It should use that strategy. It should not mind about the corridor to Mullingar, although if a bus lane was provided on that route I would be grateful. If the Government wants to develop its spatial strategy, it should fly the buggers straight to Shannon, right into the west. They would hire cars and fill the pubs.'

'We have 100 new aircraft due to be delivered to us over the next eight years. We would like to place at least 20 or 30 of those aircraft in this country. Twenty of those aircraft could be based in Dublin and 10 in Shannon. There would be no room for American military aircraft in Shannon if we had our way.'

'The advance bookings to Kerry are higher than those to Shannon. It is not that people did not want to visit Shannon. With the greatest respect, there is nothing particularly unique or attractive about Shannon per se but as a gateway to the west of Ireland, it is very attractive to

German, Italian and French visitors. So too is Kerry. The traffic and the routes will always go wherever the costs are lowest, yet the three main airports here are run by a Government-owned monopoly which, during a world-wide recession and an international war, decided it would increase costs for the only airline growing business out of Shannon. That speaks for itself.'

On the 2012 London Olympics: 'It's going to be cheaper and faster to get to London from the west of Ireland than it's going to be to get from many UK cities like Birmingham, Manchester and Liverpool. I thinks that's why a lot of teams and delegations will be looking at Shannon and the west, not just in 2012 but for training camps in 2011 and 2010.'

'Limerick is not the centre of the universe. It may be so in Irish rugby, but not in world aviation.'

BRITISH AIRPORT AUTHORITY

'I never said that Stansted is a great place.'

'The British Airport Authority are on a cocaine-induced spending spree. They are an overcharging, gold-plating monopoly which should be broken up.'

'The BAA want to spend £4 billion on an airport which should cost £100 million. £3.9 billion is for tree-planting, new roadways and Norman Foster's Noddy railway so they can mortgage away the future of low-cost airlines. This plan is for the birds. BAA are a glorified shopping mall.'

'BAA have no particular skills in building airports and are the worst airport builders in the western world.'

'The latest unjustified price hikes by the BAA airport monopoly prove that it is abusing its monopoly power over passengers and airlines at Stansted. They also prove that the CAA is an incompetent and incapable regulator which has yet again put the financial needs of the Spanish-owned BAA airport operator above the interests of airport-users and consumers, which it is obliged by law to protect.'

On building new runways at Stansted: 'I think it's about bloody time. The British need to get their act together to compete with the French and the Germans. You have to develop more runways and terminals. There's been a lot of sitting on hands over here. Far too much time and attention is paid here to environmental groups and every other not-in-my-backyard you can think of.'

'If you live around Heathrow and you don't like living beside an airport, sell the house and move. But the south-east of England needs more capacity and it is about time we got on and built it.'

On asking Stansted Airport to waive landing charges: 'What we got back from BAA was a polite two-word letter. The second word was "off". My pet pony would do a better job.'

'It is untenable for the BAA airport monopoly to impose fuel levies in excess of 300% of cost on its low-fare consumers, whilst at the same time providing free-of-charge car parking to politicians. This anti-consumer rip-off must end.'

'People can drive up the M11, they will walk barefoot over the fields for a cheap fare. What they are not going to do is pay 15 years in advance for some bloody marble Taj Mahal.'

'I could check in people in the car park, which would be cheaper than BAA. If they don't let me use their car parks we might let them check in at the truckers' car park on the M11.'

'Ryanair has long called for a break-up of the BAA monopoly. Heathrow is a shambles which most passengers, if they could, would avoid at all costs. Equally Stansted, where we operate, is an over-specified, gold-plated Taj Mahal.'

'A break-up of BAA would be the greatest thing that has happened to British aviation since the founding of Ryanair. Then airline customers would not be forced to endure the black hole of Calcutta that is Heathrow, or the unnecessary, overpriced palace being planned at Stansted.'

'Who wants to travel through Heathrow? It's a nightmare. You spend ages in queues and security checks when you could travel to Stansted with a fast train into the centre of London more cheaply and with less hassle. Equally, we aren't allowed to claim that an airport is in a city if it doesn't call itself "Frankfurt Airport". If you want to spend hundreds more pounds to not have to take a half-hour train journey then go ahead.'

'No airport is attractive on its own. Nobody flew to Stansted in 1991, yet this year the figure will be 20 million passengers. Luton, which had about one million passengers six years ago thanks to easyJet, will have about seven million passengers this year. If you have low fares you have huge traffic growth. Airports are nothing more than glorified shopping centres; they are a means of getting people quickly through.'

'Our best-selling route at Luton is Esbjerg. On these flights, 72% of the passengers are of Danish origin. Passengers are coming over on our flights to watch football—the likes of Arsenal and Chelsea. Not Luton Town, they're a shit team.'

'People in Britain deserve their holidays. And we need visitors to fly to Britain as well, or the economy will be in the toilet.'

'People stop booking flights when they see all the mess at the UK airports.'

On the BAA being bought by a Spanish company: 'They're a Johnny Foreigner. It doesn't matter whether it is a British highwayman, a Spanish highwayman or an American highwayman. You are still getting robbed and that won't change until you break BAA's monopoly up.'

'In the case of Britain's air traffic control system, they have pissed away millions, millions of our money, it was 15 years late and it doesn't work. Stop building bloody marble palaces in Portsmouth and Brussels, and give us the service we need. ATS is a shambles. These guys can't re-cruit enough people, can't train them and can't run their own systems yet now they're looking for more money.'

'We're not going to pull out of Stansted, but we're not going to be robbed there either. It's Taj Mahals, gherkins and building projects for wannabe candidates for the House of Lords. BAA should stop buying Noddy train sets which take you halfway round Essex to get you to a satellite building 60 yards away. Our passengers would prefer to walk.'

AIRPORTS

'We are a monopolist because we are able to dictate terms to airports.'

'We simply allocate the new aircraft arrivals to airports all over Europe where, quite remarkably, airports, ministers and Governments desperately vie with each other to offer us better deals, terms and facilities to get us to fly to their local airport, city or region and transform their tourism.'

'Airports are coming to us saying, "Please open a base." Usually we make a decision based on that airport providing us with a very good package of facilities and they have to be efficient facilities, at low cost. Whichever airport provides us with the best package is the next new route we open.'

'We are going all over Europe—Belgium, Germany, Spain, Norway, Sweden and Denmark—where airports are falling over themselves to give us 25-year deals. They love us in England and we're treated like gods in Europe. Our proposals are welcomed with open arms all over Europe.'

'We don't view any airport as a long-term arrangement per se. The biggest incentive for us to use an airport is a package of low charges. All our existing arrangements are interchangeable.'

'We are going to have 75–80% of our passengers checking in online early next year. Most of our passengers travel with hand luggage. When you book a ticket and print off your own boarding card, you no longer have to check in at the airport. You don't need to go through the terminal building, you don't need to pay terminal charges for check-in desks. This is the way to blow up the airport monopoly. We would save 20% of our costs, €50 million total, across the business.'

'We're in the final stages of doing a deal with a kiosk provider and we're pretty confident that in the next few years you won't have Ryanair check-in desks at all, you'll just have kiosks. We're telling airports that we want to use as few of their facilities as is humanly possible.'

'Bus operators carrying American tourists park near the tourist shops around Nassau Street. Many of those shops give the bus drivers a kick-back on the spend. I always wonder why airports do not do that. We are the bus drivers who deliver hundreds of thousands of passengers. The airports may not charge us to park outside their shops but they should give us a kick-back on the spend.'

'Without passengers the hotels do not make anything, nor does the airport. All we ask is, not so much for a freebie, but for the airport to be competitive with all the other airports around Europe.'

'Why would airports allow an airline to fly to them for free? It is because they get more out of passengers in car-parking, restaurant and shop fees and concessions.'

'It is an open fact that some airports pay us to fly there and that they are profitable. They are privately owned. People do not do this because they are Government subsidised. They are privately owned and pay us to fly there. Why? It is because they get €3 per passenger on everyone coming through.'

'Lying governments have got together with airports to rip us off. We should say, "We aren't fucking taking it any more."'

'I am not having a go at the regional airports which have to survive on their own, but there is no real demand for internal flights in this country. The demand is actually from those airports to London and other international destinations. There is no great future in developing the airports in Donegal, Sligo and Waterford. They are too small and the country cannot support them. Even Knock, despite the fact that we fly there, is pretty flaky as well.'

'Leitrim is always foremost in our minds as we develop new bases.'

On the Scottish Highlands and Islands Airport Authority:
'It's like the 1950s, you can't scratch your backside unless you get a subsidy first. It operates its airports like a tourist attraction.'

'We are not flying to airports that increase charges. I do not care if they are Shannon, Dublin or Stansted as long as there are many other airports where the costs are lower. Why do we do this? We are trying to lower costs for consumers. We want to reduce the cost of air travel. We are not bloody geniuses.'

'There's all kinds of places in Scandinavia and down through Germany where NATO had bases during the Cold

War. Even in the UK there's dozens of airports. When you look at an ordinary map you think there's no more airports; in actual fact, the place is absolutely awash with airports. We look for the signs which show there's an airport somewhere and go and talk with them.'

DESTINATIONS

'Take Gdansk. Who wants to go to Gdansk? There ain't a lot there after you've seen the shipyard wall.'

'We've never done market research on any of our new routes. We don't go in for demographic analysis. We simply look for airports with efficient facilities and a low-cost base. There are a lot of people, particularly in London, who are always looking for somewhere different. If you can fly to somewhere in Europe for under £10 then you are going to fill 200 seats a day to almost anywhere. People have laughed at some of our more unusual destinations, but we've never stopped flying to any of them due to lack of interest.'

'We haven't carried out any market research as I believe that what we offer is self-explanatory. If you can fly to the same destination with two airlines and one offers a fare which is a great deal less, then obviously you will choose the cheaper fare; there's no research needed for that.'

'It's not as if JFK was in Central Park or Heathrow was in Pall Mall. I don't give a toss where people want to go. I'm in the business of creating a market for people to go where they never have heard of. What we do is stimulate huge demand, and then capture it.'

'We had a presentation from a European Government two weeks ago. The Tourism and Transport Ministers came over and offered us a 20-year deal, with employment grants and our own terminal and everything. I had to go and meet them, though; you have to kiss someone's ass.'

'There was a proposal to build an airport in Abbeyshrule and various other places. Ireland has a population of 3.5 million people and it has 11 airports and four airlines. Bristol has a population of 10 million people within a catchment area of one hour of that city, yet it has only one airport and no airlines. We are over-supplied with airports here.'

'Cork is Mickey Mouse stuff. Do we care about Cork? Frankly, no. Bristol is bigger than Cork; nearly everything is bigger than Cork. The reality for Cork Airport is they put up costs and they lost passengers, and that will cost them. Get them to explain how that makes fucking business sense.'

'With regard to considering developing our operation at Knock, we will continue to consider it, but the difficulty with it is that it is not a place where we could base aircraft. To base aircraft one needs good weather and to be able to get an aircraft out early in the morning and back in late in the evening. The weather in Knock is bad. Leeds Bradford is another airport where we cannot base an aircraft. The weather is poor there. We can get in and out of Knock pretty regularly with mid-morning and mid-afternoon flights. We would never get in and out of it early in the morning or late at night. With regard to whether Knock is a possible access point for low-fare services to the west, it is absolutely and I have no difficulty with that. With regard to whether we would want to own an airport in the midlands, we would not for the same weather reason. The midlands is bedevilled with fog. I know that because I drive from there early in the morning and return late in the evening. For some reason Mullingar always seems to get fog.'

'We would like to do more and base more aircraft here in Belfast and are working with the City Airport to get the runway extended. Let's get the planning permission through and let's ignore the mewling and puking from local residents which is a load of nonsense.'

'Glasgow Prestwick was very much like Shannon and until the mid-1960s relied on the transatlantic stop-over traffic. It had about two and a half million passengers per year. Prior to 1997 when we started to fly there out of Dublin, it had no passengers. The airport had been closed and there were sheep on the runway. This year traffic at Prestwick will be somewhere north of two million passengers. The reason that is important is that it is a model for what can be done at Shannon Airport. If we can deliver two million passengers to a place in the west of Scotland which had sheep on the runway, we can deliver to some place in the west of Ireland where if nothing intelligent is done, there will be sheep on the runway when the peace protesters and the American military are gone.'

'Liverpool is the low-fares regional airport for the north-west of England. Liverpool doesn't have all the glass, bells and whistles that Manchester has, but passengers don't want glass, bells and whistles. It's always good to see Liverpool give Manchester a good kicking.'

'We can't get Birmingham Airport to wake up, which is a tragedy.'

'Newquay is the surf and dope capital of Britain. There's next to frig-all way of getting to Cornwall unless you fly. It's a fucking impossible nine-day hike. Closing that airport would be a disaster for surfer dudes, but also to loads of wealthy types who use us to commute up and down. I tell you, we'll have a bloody dogfight with the RAF. Watch out for those 737s on your wing, flyboys.'

'Brussels Charleroi is the secondary airport for Brussels. I am sorely tempted to say that nobody in this Dáil committee room would know much about it since most politicians and civil servants still fly with Aer Lingus to Brussels Zaventem.'

'When we started flying into Pau house prices tripled.'

'Frankfurt-Hahn Airport is 100 kilometres outside Frankfurt. Everybody said it would not work. It was a former NATO military base. The military had pulled out and there were no customers left. We went in there. They have built a new terminal for us. We will carry three million passengers per year to and from an airport where, three years ago, there were no passengers at all.'

'What makes Frankfurt-Hahn different is that everything they said they would do from day one they have delivered on. They are charging us a very low cost per passenger. I would not tell my mother how much. It is an immaterial sum of money on a per-passenger basis.'

'I was told to go to Malta because there is all-year-round sunshine, and the moment I step off the plane it starts raining. That's it, I'm pulling my airline out of Malta.'

'Would we have a base in Athens? It's too far away from everywhere else, so no. Would we have a base in Malta? No. But would we do a route down to Athens if we could get a low-cost base at an Athenian airport? Yes, we probably would. Longer flights won't stop us going into those markets. We're not going to leave the markets out there.'

'Twelve months ago I believed it made no sense flying to Poland. I've changed my mind. We will have 1 million passengers on our routes to Poland. We're happy to let our higher-cost rivals get in there. We will follow when the time is right. We'll then push the others out to Russia, then Siberia.'

On new routes: 'We never want to be the explorers; they always get their heads shot off.'

On distant destinations: 'People won't pay four times more for flights that are four times longer, so fuck that.'

PUBLICITY

'Habemus lowest fares, my children.'

'All we do is go around, create a bit of controversy, do silly things, get our photograph taken in silly places and reduce the advertising money, and like that we can afford to keep the prices down.'

'You've got to keep people interested. We specialise in cheap publicity stunts.'

'If you have low fares, you have to shout your mouth off a lot more.'

'If you make a lot of noise and fight with a lot of people you generate a lot of cheap publicity.'

'That's the downside of being a no-frills airline: you have to take cheap advertising where you can get it.'

'We prefer to dole out bons mots at regular weekly intervals.'

'Usually someone gets offended by our ads, which is fantastic. You get a whole lot more bang for your buck if somebody is upset.'

'Bookings peak for big advertisements. And they'll peak even more if somebody reacts badly to the advertisement.'

On dressing as St Patrick at a 17 March press conference: 'Step this way, my children. I'm hoping to wind things up as quick as possible so I can have a few beers back in Dublin.'

On dressing as Caesar in Rome: 'They're not used to someone going down and making a complete tit of himself.'

'I don't mind dressing up in something stupid or pulling gormless faces if it helps. Frankly, I don't give a rat's arse about my personal dignity.'

'You cannot on the one hand court publicity as I do for Ryanair and then on the other hand say, "Oh, I want to be alone." But it's a small price to pay.'

'If you live by the sword, you have to accept the occasional slash yourself.'

'I'm not doing something new as Richard Branson did it for years.'

'We're doing what Branson did in the UK 20 years ago. You can make a lot of PR bang for your buck by being a little bit wacky.'

'I try desperately not to get into the Branson stuff. This is not O'Leary Air.'

On an advert depicting the Pope claiming that the fourth secret of Fatima was Ryanair's low fares, to which the Vatican accused the airline of blaspheming the Pope, generating even more publicity: 'I thought I died and went to heaven.'

'You don't need to be infallible to know that only Ryanair guarantees the lowest fares to Rome. Ryanair's new route means it's black smoke from now on for Aer Lingus's high prices.'

'I wouldn't believe anything I read in the Irish Times.'

On consumer magazine 'Which?': 'I think you'd find more relevant consumer information in the Beano or the Dandy than in this magazine.'

On adding bigger breasts to the lady on the aircraft tail: 'She looked like a bloke with wings. Somebody said we should give her bigger boobs. So we did. Some quango said we were demeaning women. Fuck off. She's got bigger boobs. And the story got two half-pages in The Sun, worth £25,000 each.'

'Everyone here is delighted that our employee Brian Dowling made it into the Channel 4 Big Brother house. He's been two years in the Ryanair madhouse, which is perfect training. We will be holding his job for him and hope that he will be returning to us, unless, of course, he becomes an international superstar through this.'

When Dowling won: 'I don't imagine he will want to come back if he is making a fortune. If he does, then we would be glad to have him, and perhaps we would use him in promotions. But if he is looking for appearance money he can feck off.'

On the Advertising Standards Authority: 'They say, "You're screwing people, because all the cheap seats are available on the shitty days when people don't want to go and then charging high prices on the Friday and Saturday." Well, the first 15% or 20% of people to book for Friday and Saturday get the cheapest prices. We have those prices available every day, and usually on every flight. But we're giving away tickets at stupid prices when people don't want to fly. We have to make money somewhere.'

After paying an £18,000 fine to the Advertising Standards Authority: 'All advertising is now vetted by three different people in the company, not only because we do not want to mislead consumers, but because we do not want to waste £18,000.'

On negative press comments after 9/11: 'Screw them. People have been offended by our ads before and that doesn't bother us. What we're about is not lying down in front of these terrorists and letting them win. The tragedy that happened in the US was bad publicity and it affected consumer confidence. Safety is always an issue in the airline industry and that is one of the things on which we would not try to seek publicity. But most other things are fair game: politicians, popes. What we are trying to do is run ads that get noticed, that are controversial and that will get people to pick up the phone and book flights. Our ads are so successful, it's almost scary.'

'We got into horse racing because there are strong Irish links with Cheltenham. There is an annual exodus of drunken Paddies coming for four days of gambling and other recreation. If you went on Google and stuck in "Ryanair chase" you'd get 216,000 worldwide media references to it. That's an equivalent of €3.2 million in advertising value to us. It's absurd, for one poxy race meeting in the Cotswolds. It makes no sense that one race on one course in the Cotswolds in England should deliver that kind of international noise but it does and it's great value for money. Jump racing may have a narrow focus on Northern Europe but it has the international audience that Ryanair is looking for. We look for opportunities that people don't expect. From the start of May, people are talking about the festival that happens in March the following year, which is a lot of time for your brand. Other sports are outrageously expensive for what they deliver. If you're sponsoring behind the corner flag at some football ground, you'll pay much more for a lot less value. Formula One is a classic example. You pay a couple of million for a tiny logo behind the wheel to be exposed to a worldwide television audience of 2.2 billion—none of whom can see your bloody brand.'

To the City Diary editor at the Guardian: 'I realise that figures, accuracy and your good self have long been strangers. Everything in yesterday's diary item about Ryanair was wrong. I love the column, we must keep this going.'

With Ryanair's marketing manager, Sinéad Finn, addressing an all-male press conference when she said, 'I've got nine men in front of me. I don't know where to start.' 'They're hardly all men. One of them is from the *Guardian*.'

At a press conference in Germany and on being asked about a possible new transatlantic airline: 'There will be a business class and an economy class. And the economy class will be very cheap, we said €10 across the Atlantic, but the business class will be very expensive. In business class it will be beds and blow jobs. In business class it will all be free—including the blow jobs. What's the German for blow job? There is no German for blow job? Terrible sex life in Germany.'

At a press conference, about a female reporter who, trying not to interrupt him, crawled towards his desk to retrieve her microphone: 'If you want to stay on your knees, by all means, I'd encourage you. Sorry, I've forgotten the question. There was a very pretty girl on her knees there in front of me.'

'Welcome to the Ryanair press conference, the only press conference where you can identify the person who is lying because his lips are moving. Everyone at a press conference is telling lies. I thought that was the first rule of journalism school. We had the first press conference since the bank holiday and I thought we'd have the whole day to ourselves. And then fucking M&S goes and sacks someone. It's only women's knickers. Relax.'

At an over-hyped press conference: 'I'm a bit disturbed the rumour went round we would announce my resignation and the share price rose 3%.'

On being accused of blatant plugs for Ryanair's low fares live on BBC News 24: 'I can't help it.'

At a Ryanair Annual General Meeting, to a grey-haired shareholder who expressed disquiet at the age of some of Ryanair's planes: 'This is a shareholder, I take it! What age are you, Sir? It ill behoves you to be criticising clapped-out 20-year-olds.'

On being photographed with old ladies at an Annual General Meeting: 'My favourite shareholders. This girl is my boss.'

'What are you going to ask me about next? Sex? Religion?'

Halfway through a first-quarter results media presentation, aged 41, when his mobile phone rang: 'It was my mother. She wanted to know where I was.'

'As long as it's not safety-related, there's no such thing as bad publicity.'

CHANNEL 4 'DISPATCHES' PROGRAMME

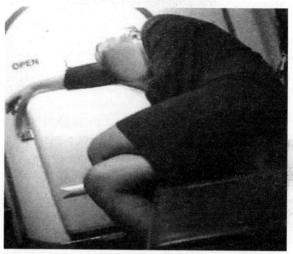

'It's a posed "set-up" taken in some other airline's air-craft.'

'This posed photograph, which purports to be a Ryanair aircraft, is as manufactured as the rest of the evidence which has so far been provided by Dispatches to Ryanair.'

'We have replied to all allegations made and have copied all of this correspondence at every stage to the relevant aviation regulatory authorities in the UK and Ireland and they have also confirmed that they can find no substance to any of these written allegations on the basis of the evidence thus far produced by Dispatches.'

'If that's the best they can do after five months, then they should give up filming.'

'Channel 4 can shove this programme up its jacksie.'

'This is not a documentary. It's more like a soap. The public have more common sense than a sensationalised TV programme. There's nothing in it.'

'There's sick bags on board the aircraft and lots of cloths. If there's a very bad one, you call the cleaners at the airport. It's no big issue. How long does it take to clean up some sick?'

'We got the rosters for the two journalists who'd been working for the three months. One averaged 36 hours a week, one 28 hours. They filmed one in her flat late at night who, crying and whispering, claimed to have been at work since 4 a.m. and just got back at 8 p.m. Rubbish. We have maximum duty days of 14 hours. She never did it.'

'What you're left with is two journalists, one of whom was working a four-day week and the other working a 3½ day week—which I accept for journalists is a very busy week.'

'We held an Oscars night but it wasn't for the press, it was for staff. Either the staff would be sitting at home worried that they were going to be sacked, or we could deal with it the best way we know how. So we said, "Right, we're going to have a free bar; everybody comes in and nobody gets fired." We were not going on a witch-hunt. And it was great.'

'We're doing a follow-up. We have pulled in all of our cabin crew trainers this week. We've sat down with the safety instructors and we've gone to the handling agents. And we sold 20,000 extra seats yesterday.'

TAXI

'I have a taxi because it's a good investment.'

'I was sitting there in traffic one day. The Government had deregulated the taxis and I saw that taxis could use the bus lane. There's a bus lane and it would save me half an hour coming into the office in the morning. And I'm thinking, why don't I?'

'At a time when there is a about to be a war in Iraq and there is a crisis in the health service, Michael O'Leary's taxi is capable of exciting everyone.'

'It's a black taxi registered in Mullingar. I have a driver who drives it for me. I own the car. I own the plate and I operate a taxi, as do 12,000 other people in Ireland.'

'Nobody would argue that the deregulation of the taxi industry in Dublin in recent months has not at least improved the availability of taxis. I speak with some expertise in this.'

'As far as I understand it, people are upset because my taxi uses a bus lane on the way to Dublin Airport. But if I rent a taxi in Mullingar he can drive up the bus lane to Dublin Airport and there is no problem. If you're in Mullingar then give me a call. I'd be happy to look after you.'

'Last time I checked this was a democratic republic. As long as I pay my taxes I'm free to do with my money what I like. It costs me more to get from Mullingar than to fly to London, but that is neither here nor there.'

'If they want to amend the taxi regulations which say I'm allowed to pick up people in Dublin, I'll be happy to pick up people in Dublin. And I'll do it a lot cheaper.'

'There is a meter in the taxi and it produces receipts. The fare from Mullingar to Dublin Airport is €80. We are a low-cost airline so we wouldn't entertain mileage allowances like that.'

'Everyone expects you to be all humble and ashamed. Bollocks. I bought the plate, it operates perfectly legally. It picks me up, it drops me off.'

'I have a Mercedes 500. Not because I like the Mercedes 500, but because it's a big, comfortable fucking car.'

'I was always a transport innovator. I always like to be at the cutting edge of transport solutions.'

On being convicted and fined for dangerous driving: 'I'm very sorry; I feel the court was very fair, the judge was very fair, the guards were very fair and the two people who gave evidence were very fair. I will try and learn from the experience. I clearly made a mistake. I'm sorry to have wasted the Garda and court time.'

'The taxi was the best six grand I ever spent. A helicopter would be a little over the top.'

LOVE

'It was a chance for me to dress up with a couple of pretty girls. It's a shitty job but someone has to do it.'

'I spent from 20 to 40 working like a black. I can bloody say that. I used to work seven days a week and usually 16-hour days. I had no time for girlfriends. I didn't have girlfriends for 10 or 15 years. I generally get on very well with women.'

'I'd love to spend the rest of my life on a beach in Barbados with a load of babes, but I'm striking out badly on that front.'

On his early interests: 'Smoking, drinking, and chasing loose women.'

Before being married: 'I breed horses and cattle. It's the closest thing I have to a sex life. I spare no expense on the bulls, but now if only I could find a woman.'

'I have this theory that childbirth is so frightening, and you're so involved in it, that it's probably not very positive. But delivering a calf, well, that's fucking amazing.'

On cancelling his first wedding: 'I'm not gay, before you ask. I crashed and burnt. I came very close to finding the one but it didn't happen, so it's kick on and just go back to work. I am depressingly single and I am living in hope that a woman will find me sufficiently attractive to settle down.'

On meeting his wife: 'It was at a wedding that I was brutally dragged to because it was one of the Ryans. She was a bridesmaid and she took pity on me.'

'Aunty fucking Mavis? Who the fuck is Aunty fucking Mavis? My bride-to-be keeps asking which I would prefer about wedding things I don't really have an opinion about either way. That's what I try and say, but it always comes out sounding like I don't give a fuck.'

'The wedding reception is going to be cheap. The honeymoon is going to kill me. We are going to Ryanair destinations, so at least I can get back quickly. No press. You must be joking. I'm only having friends at this reception.'

On his bride arriving 35 minutes late for their wedding: 'She's coming here with Aer Lingus.'

At his wedding: 'I'm terrified. I've never been so nervous in my whole life.'

'I never thought about selling my wedding to Hello! That's for the ones who can't afford to pay for their own weddings.'

'I didn't want a bunch of politicians at my wedding for the sake of having politicians at my wedding. I know Charlie and Noleen McCreevy. I know Mary and Brian Harney, so they got invited. And I know JP McManus for donkeys years—if you were involved in racing then you know JP. There were no celebs there.'

'We threw out the last guest at 6.30 in the morning. We'd laid on low-fare buses to get them home. I guarantee I won't be selling shares this year. The wedding got paid for so I'm all right.'

On whether marriage would make him more mellow: 'I don't think so. I hope not.'

'I have just had the first child. My experience of five weeks of fatherhood is that I want to spend more time at the office. I am staying in the guest room and I don't plan to re-emerge until my son is at least two years old and ready to take instructions. I'm taking the company approach to it: I am subcontracting everything.'

'I changed the first nappy in the hospital and, called upon in emergency, I will do another. I'm not one of these people who will be there doing the full-time father lark.'

'My experience of most married men is that after marriage and children they tend to spend more time at the office than they did before. The record of most men I know is that they tend to work harder when they're married. I think getting married will ultimately change your lifestyle and it's taken me a long time to find the right woman anyway.'

On what keeps him up at night: 'My wife and two young children.'

'Since I got married I usually take one holiday during the year but if I can avoid it I will.'

'I'm a fat cat when I fly in business class on long-haul flights. Otherwise I am not a fat cat. I am actually quite a slim cat. But my wife disagrees with that.'

'I was rude, worked too hard, I am probably a bit offensive. I am certainly not charming. I don't do nightclubs. I was too busy working through my thirties to meet someone. I got very lucky, met someone lovely. I couldn't be happier. I have been happier this week than at any time in 15 years.'

Using the F-word 14 times at a press conference: 'I am in the first year of marriage. We've had our first row. She wanted to know where I was going to be in a week's time. How do I know that?'

On addressing students at Trinity College, Dublin: 'I'm not visiting because of some undying loyalty to Trinity. I'm here because of the high percentage of hot undergraduate totty in the room. When I was in college, none of you would have looked at me twice, but now you're going to have to sit here and listen to me for an hour.'

When waiting to enter the Trinity hall, and taking a call on his mobile phone where he was informed that Rimini Airport had demanded increased landing fees: 'Tell them to fuck off.'

On introducing a management pay freeze: 'Someone's just frozen my effing pay. I'm trying to keep it quiet. I might have to tell my wife that we've got to cut back, that she'll have to start shopping at Lidl or Aldi rather than Tesco. The major sufferer here will be Mrs Willie Walsh. Mrs O'Leary may suffer as a consequence but she'll just have to tighten her belt for a year or two.'

On a business poll where women rated him less favourably than men did: 'I have spent my whole life trying to increase my ratings with the ladies. Sadly, this survey confirms that it was all a waste of time.'

On RTÉ radio when selecting his three favourite pieces of music ('Jerusalem' sung by the Winchester Cathedral Choir, 'Stay' by U2 and 'The Power of Love' by Frankie Goes to

Hollywood (his wife's favourite song and danced to at his wedding)): 'If you had asked me I would have given you three pieces of music by U2, but that would have been fairly boring. If you went to Trinity in the early 1980s and you are in your mid-40s in Ireland and you are not a lifelong U2 fan then you should be shot. They are one of the great adverts for modern Ireland. They haven't blown it. They are one of the greatest things Ireland has produced in the last 30 years, apart from Ryanair.'

'Kenneth Williams had it right. Infamy, infamy, they fucking have it in for me.'

On business: 'It's economics. It's not society. I don't do bonding.'

'I will trip up at some stage. I'm not God; I might like to think I'm God, but I'm not.'

'I am very humble, shy and retiring. It is my humility that makes me the success I am today and also the fact that I am caring helps too.'

'I'm a genius, but I'm just too humble to say so.'

'I'm certainly er... memorable; some people think I am arrogant and a loudmouth, which in some cases would be hard to argue against, and—er—foul-mouthed. I don't wear a suit, which is not some Bransonesque thing that I never wear a suit, I just don't like coming to work in a suit.'

'I frankly don't care what people say about me or write about me. I didn't get into this job for the popularity. I'm only concerned about what the people in this airline think about me.'

'I'm probably just an obnoxious little bollocks. Who cares? The purpose is not to be loved. The purpose is to have the passengers on board.'

HOME

'My house itself isn't massive.'

'I grew up on a farm and I'd always known that if I ever got any money I wanted to have my own house, my own farm. Then I got lucky and got more money and I wanted a grander house.'

'I was probably put to the pin of my collar to pay for my house. I had spent a couple of hundred thousand that I didn't really have doing it up, and so the tax relief was very important to me at the time. People think I pulled out of the tax relief scheme because I am a celebrity. I didn't. I pulled out of the scheme five years earlier because at that stage I thought, I want to get married and have a family down here. It's not so much that I don't want them coming into my family home; frankly, I don't much care. But it's not fair to your future wife and kids to have people traipsing up and down the place for three months in the summer.'

'People go on about this magnificent mansion. It's a very nice family home. It's not one of those big palatial mansions, nor was it built to be. It was built as a weekend home for someone in Dublin, but on a grand scale. I wouldn't want my kids rattling around in a ginormous fucking mansion.'

'My house isn't small but it feels fairly compact. If you have kids and the kids are growing up and bringing friends back, you don't want them to think they are arriving in Buckingham Palace.'

'With one 18-month-old at home and another on the way, I've got plenty to keep me busy. I love working on the farm, playing tennis and having my family around me.'

'I don't like to go abroad on holiday. I don't like sunshine. When I can stay at home in Ireland, what the hell would I want to go away for?'

'I work my ass off six days a week, 12-hour days. I commute one hour to get here. I haven't got some bucolic lifestyle. Having grown up on a farm I would like my family to grow up on a farm. Like most people today I need to work harder and harder to make wealth for my family. I live in great fear of spending my 80 years and not making a difference. Even if you only pissed people off at least you made a difference.'

'I'm an Irish peasant at heart. I grew up on a farm in the Irish countryside, and now I live on a farm in the Irish countryside. You would impress fucking nobody if you drove to the paper shop on a Sunday morning in your Ferrari. They'd think you were a gobshite. And you probably would be. A big tractor, now, they might be impressed. But it doesn't get to the shop fast enough for me.'

'My hobby is agriculture. That's perhaps what I will do for a few years.'

'The word "buggers" is a term of endearment in Mullingar.'

'I didn't want to be in Charolais bulls because Tony Ryan and Tony O'Reilly and all those guys were into Charolais. I didn't want to be pricking around as the latest idiot with his Charolais cows.'

'I wanted something which was a native breed to Ireland, which means Whitehorns or Angus. The Angus were easy calving, they are very easy to handle. For someone who farms two days a week they were perfect. I spent one week on a course about Low-Cost Artificial Insemination Techniques for Angus Heifers. Frankly, it was a load of bull.'

'I drive the tractors and the quads sometimes. Oh, and I like antique furniture and paintings, but I don't spend too much on them. I haven't really got the time—I'm always working.'

On a prize bull: 'All he does is makes babies and eat. That's what I look forward to doing when I retire.'

On buying a €42,000 prize bull: 'As you know I have a long-standing policy of not commenting on rumour or speculation, regardless of how much bullshit is involved.'

'I'm always polite.'

'I never comment on anything to do with my private life. And that's private, sorry. Look, I'll answer any question on Ryanair, but when it comes to myself the answer is, "There is no answer."'

SPORT

'There are great people in horse racing and there are messers.'

'I fell off a horse at the age of four and I realised it was a stupid activity. My brothers and sisters didn't realise how stupid it was and kept going.'

'If my brother Eddie wasn't involved, I wouldn't be involved. You want to be up early in the morning to be ahead of the guys in the Irish bloodstock industry. Eddie is the judge. He decides what we buy or don't buy. It's important to have someone like that. Someone you can trust. It's like any walk of life. Eddie's advice is vital.'

'Death and injuries are what I hear most of the time. It's very hard to take. But it's what you have to accept as part and parcel of the game. If you can't deal with them, you shouldn't be in it. The number of horses I own now hovers around 20, but in the last two years, four of my five best have been killed.'

'It's 90% frustration and 10% fun. But the 10% fun vastly outweighs the other side. The owner is the mug at the bottom of the food chain. As long as you know that, you'll be okay. But you have to know you will lose your money. Which makes me an idiot.'

'I keep a couple of race horses but that's kind of chump change. I don't know enough about them to be able to train them or ride them or anything like that.'

'As a businessman, I can make plans and I can have influence, but in jump racing I have to accept that the owner is merely the idiot at the bottom of the pile. The trainer and the jockeys make all the important decisions; I just pay the bills.'

'But if you like the people in jump racing, as I do, then the sport becomes a great social activity. It's a perfect pursuit for stupid rich guys.'

'In five years, we expect to be carrying 100 million passengers, which we hope will keep our share price flying and keep me in racehorses, which is the only reason I go to work anyway.'

'The Cheltenham Festival is a great Irish institution—for me, the Olympics of racing, although still an occasion to be routinely beaten up by the English.'

At Cheltenham: 'I am not sobbing over these politicians' mad, insane new environmental policies. I am just cross that my horses are doing so badly. One was last, one was second last. That's far more important, don't you think? I came to Cheltenham on Ryanair with 188 other Irish passengers. The plane was full.'

'I've learned not to have any firm hopes heading into Cheltenham, since the moment you start hoping is the moment your horse is likely to get injured. At

Cheltenham, it's an achievement just to have a horse running, so to have a winner this year would be beyond my wildest expectations. I suppose my first winner is about five or six years away.'

When his horse War of Attrition won the Cheltenham Gold Cup: 'Unbelievable, I've died and gone to heaven. I've been owning horses for around 10 years and never did I dream of winning the Cheltenham Gold Cup. My brother Eddie, who bought War Of Attrition for me, always thought he was good enough but I never did. I'd be more nervous at a point-to-point than I was today. We died out there last year. As I watched the race it was like it was happening in slow motion. The last few furlongs took about two hours. All I kept saying to myself was "Please be over. Please be over." The good Lord shines down on some of us. It's just wonderful. I'm floating on air. Free flights for everyone this evening. I'll pay for them all myself. Tonight we shall have a couple of very quiet drinks soberly before catching the 9 p.m. Ryanair to Twickenham to watch Ireland beat England. On time too. And we'll be paying for our luggage.'

When War of Attrition won the Guinness Gold Cup at Punchestown: 'We've a very good horse and a very cool jockey. I was incredibly nervous today. At Cheltenham, we didn't expect anything, but today we half-expected it.'

'I'd love to win the Grand National. I remember as a kid bunking off from school to put money on the Grand National. I wouldn't be a big punter. I'd say the biggest bet I've had was 50 quid. The bet was each way. It's the accountant in me. You can take the man out of accountancy but you can't take the accountant out of the man.'

When his horse Hear The Echo won the Irish Grand National: 'We had no money on him. Two people asked me earlier should they back him and I told them no way. I thought he was going out for a run to keep himself warm.'

On receiving the Irish Grand National Trophy from the Taoiseach: 'I don't get much off Bertie Ahern, but I'll take the cup for the Grand National off him any time.'

'I am from Westmeath and our footballers never get their retaliation in first. That is why Meath beats us every year.'

'When I was younger I dreamed of playing football for Manchester City.'

'I've followed Manchester City closely since the late 1960s—an experience rather like jump racing, really, in that the good days are far outnumbered by the bad and you have to learn to take your beatings.'

'They wanted me to buy Manchester City a year ago. They wanted me to buy a controlling stake. No, I did not even think about it. I got a letter last year from someone who said that they had 30% of Manchester City, wanting to know would I be interested in buying their share. They had heard I was a fan. I wrote back a very nice letter saying, "Thank you very much, I've been a lifelong supporter of Man City. They've broken my heart on numerous occasions but I'll confine my support to going to Maine Road about twice a year."'

'Can you imagine buying a controlling interest in an English soccer team? You'd be all over the back pages of the papers. That is not what running Ryanair is about. You'd be giving interviews about dealing with players' agents. It's completely insane. I confine my insanities to horse racing, which at least is relatively cheap—cheap in the context of football teams.'

'I think a right-wing dictatorship led by me would not only improve the Irish economy but the Irish football team too. Have you noticed that one way you can win the World Cup is to have a right-wing dictatorship?'

'As for England's chances in the World Cup, I'm not sure—I think when push comes to shove, you simply have a spineless team. In the Republic of Ireland's case, I think it's probably a good thing we're sitting this World Cup out. Without Roy Keane, we wouldn't have had a prayer.'

'We're Irish—we're used to losses. England come over and kick the shit out of us nine years out of 10. An age-old Irish custom is to give an English guy a kick when he's on the ground.'

WEALTH

'Don't make me look like a boring bastard in a suit.'

'I was always driven and I was always competitive. Maybe I was kicked by somebody at some stage, but if I was I don't remember it. Why are you the way you are? I haven't a bloody bull's notion. Would I want to spend a lot of time analysing myself? No.'

'I think you make things happen. But an awful lot of things happen, and not because you are in control of them. The harder you work, the luckier you get. You make your own breaks.'

'If you work hard, good things happen to you eventually. Most people who do well, generally it's a by-product of about 99% perspiration and 1% inspiration; in my case probably less inspiration and even more perspiration.'

On what makes him tick: 'The Lord alone knows. I'm not interested in myself. I'm not interested in all this psychoanalytical waffle. Money, wine and the pursuit of loose women. Money is no longer the driving force. I don't come to work because I need to put food on the table for my family. I come to work because it's fun. It's far better than poncing around on a beach somewhere.'

'I thought the first £1 million was going to be like multiple orgasms, greatest night of your life. But nothing. So you think, "I've got to double this and make two." Then four, then eight. At a certain point, don't ask when it is, money stops being important.'

'Money is important when you are trying to make the first million, 10 million, maybe the first 50 million. After that it doesn't so much matter. If you take it all away tomorrow, I will be really pissed off. Racehorses and cattle are my poison, but I don't live a high life.'

'The market has driven the share price crazy. It's a little on the high side, even though our earnings will ultimately justify it. It's a bit overheated; as the largest shareholder, I don't have a conflict of interest in saying that.'

'I'm in the tragic position of selling 10% of my holding in Ryanair a year and still having 90% of my wealth tied up in this airline. I'm selling shares for good, boring portfolio management reasons. It doesn't make sense to have everything tied up in one asset. I took a bit off last year. I'm taking a bit off now and I'll probably take a bit more off again this time next year.'

'I've sold €250 million worth of shares in the last six years and today I think I have €300 million of shares left. I thought it was time to get the hell out before the stock market crashed. Then the market upturned, which just goes to show what a moron I am. I stuck it in the post office. The money is spread around banks and post offices. I'm using it to stanch my farming losses.'

'Some people may be unhappy with the share sales. That's fine. Some people think the management should be locked in indentured fucking slavery for ever.'

'I don't want to be like the dot-com fucking goons. My policy is that I'm going to take a lump off the table every year. Dot-coms were the biggest demonstration of asinine stupidity. They were all running around being billionaires on paper and nobody took money off the table.'

'I whack it into the bank. There's nothing to manage. From a personal point of view I want some certainty that I have some cash sitting in the post office if, God forbid, terrorists blow up the London airports or we make a complete dog's balls of this operation.'

'Aviation is littered with people who stayed in for far too long and lost a fortune.'

'I do buy the occasional oil painting. I like portraits and pictures of horses. I'm not a serious collector of paintings. I buy them because I like them, but I wouldn't be frugal about it.'

'I get portrayed as being "anti" the environment, but my passion is farming. I'm all pro-environment, but I'm all for taking effective, sensible measures to enhance the environment. I've looked at a lot of potential investments in the area of clean technology and renewable energy, and I have invested in wind energy technology twice.'

'Just look at the state of the property market in Ireland. It's been crazy for the last few years and there will be some great bargains to be had in the next year or two.'

'I might leave it all to someone in the pub so they could have the biggest party in the history of Christendom. At least they would get more out of it than I did.'

'Too many people make a few quid and spend more time managing their wealth than running the company. I have a lot invested in this company. It is much more important to manage that.'

'I've paid lots of tax, unlike some people. I haven't done a lot with it. People get distracted when they put little bits in technology companies here and there. I don't want to do that. I don't want to be one of the Dublin business elite. I'm just a poor farmer from Westmeath—well, maybe not that poor. Denis O'Brien and Dermot Desmond can have all that.'

'With the amount of tax that I've paid in the last couple of years, Jesus, I've paid for my own airport by now. I paid over €20 million last year. But who wants to live in Monaco when you can live in Mullingar? It has so much more to offer. Although in all honesty, if you were being asked to pay 60% or 70% in tax, I'd be gone in a flash.'

On handing over a cheque for tax for €14 million: 'This is the most expensive stunt I've ever pulled. Paying my taxes is the price I pay for the privilege of living in the independent republic of Mullingar. I am paying enormous amounts of tax to a Government that won't make decisions on behalf of competition and consumers, but this is just a fraction of the money which is being lost to Ireland by Bertie's Government's dithering.'

'I never take helicopters; I don't trust the things; I'm terrified of them.'

On dress sense: 'People think I do this because I'm some sort of a rebel, but it's not. It's just very easy to get up in the morning and find a blue shirt and a pair of jeans. You don't have to think.'

'Do we carry rich people on our flights? Yes—I flew on one this morning and I'm very rich.'

SUCCESSION

'I am sadly and depressingly replaceable and dispensable.'

'I'm good at doing the loud-mouth and fighting everyone but it will be inappropriate to have somebody here shouting, swearing, abusing the competition. We will need more professional management than me. And that time is coming.'

'I am just a big-mouth on top of a fantastic group of people. I think it is shite to say that I am indispensable. The company stands on its own. It may have needed me 10 years ago. There is a much deeper, wider management team at this company now than me.'

'In the future the company will need a chief executive who is different than I am. As the biggest carrier in Europe, they would have no use for someone who runs around in jeans and calls politicians idiots and says that the EU Commission is made up of Communists.'

'I think we have been well served by my approach to European bureaucrats and Government taxation and stuff like that. Thus far, I think there's probably another couple of years in that.'

'At a certain point, it becomes right. In many ways I have been one of their strengths, and one of their weaknesses. In growing business, you need someone pugilistic, calling regulators gobshites, you need that hucksterism when you are building something small into something big. But when you are big, you need a different relationship with Government and regulators. I don't think that is me. You have to know when the entrepreneurial gobshite has to go.'

'At some point in time in the future the company will replace me. I suspect it won't be in the near term future, although I don't doubt there are people who would like to see me resign or fired.'

On whether the Ryanair share price will fall once he leaves: 'Many would also argue that it would rise. If I was worth anything to the share price, I wouldn't have been doing my job properly. This business doesn't depend on me any more—maybe it did 10 years ago, but not now.'

'There's a young management team. They will want to take over. It's a question for the board of Ryanair, but there are very good candidates. There's Michael Cawley and Howard Miller, both of whom would make excellent CEOs. They have been working with me for years.'

'I'm nearly certain I won't be here in five years' time. I think it'll be partly staleness, partly boredom. I think it will be time for a change in here. There are good people coming through the system here; they need to be able to see there's something. There are about four guys on the senior management team here who could run this place tomorrow morning.'

'It keeps me sane. If I was just to think, "I'm 43 and I'll be here for the next 20 years," I'd rather be shot now.'

On whether his successor will be Irish: 'Much more likely a ghastly, emollient Englishman, probably with a knighthood: Sir Roger Mucknsmuck.'

'The best businesses have a logical sequence of succession. One of the weaknesses of the company now is it is a bit cheap and cheerful and overly nasty and that reflects my personality.'

RETIREMENT

'I'll be fifty!'

'I will retire some time after we have established world domination; then it will be time for me to go. I will leave the airline when it's not growing rapidly and when it's getting dull and boring.'

'I get this every couple of years—when are you going to step down? I said probably in the next couple of years, but there are a couple of issues I want to sort out first. Frankly, if I had a competing terminal at Dublin Airport and the break-up of the London airport monopoly then I think it would be an appropriate time to go. We would like to kick off the next revolution.'

'Of course I'm only here if the shareholders want me, but I don't plan to go anywhere.'

'When I have stuffed British Airways, then I'll quit.'

'We all talk about leaving within a year here.'

On starting a new long-haul low-cost service: 'We've been approached by a number of airports in the US who are keen to see us start a long-haul, low-fare service and we're working on plans to start flying the Atlantic. There are a lot of investors who are keen to see a low-fare airline operate a transatlantic service and money is the last thing we'll need. I will personally have some say in the way it's run. By mid-2009 Ryanair will be carrying 70 million passengers at 23 bases across Europe. It will be relatively straightforward for us to do a deal for 40 to 50 long-haul aircraft and connect these bases transatlantically. There would be no one to touch us. It's a small retirement project. I do see an opportunity in four or five years' time, in the next downturn for long-haul, for a fleet of 30 or 40 aircraft. But it specifically won't be Ryanair. It may be some kind of sister company, similar investors, similar shareholders, something like that. Business class will have limo pick-ups and an onboard masseuse. I would invest in it, get it off the ground and make it fly. I would have the wrong image for sexy business class. People would say, "O'Leary will charge you for reclining your seat." But if you're going to run a long-haul airline with a business-class, first-class product, I don't think you can have me marketing it because I'm too attached—certainly in European minds—to being cheap and cheerful. But I'm thinking of calling the airline something sexy like O'Leary Air or Ego Air. Don't forget, though, this is still just a plan that hinges on us finding some cheap long-haul aircraft in a downturn. My role would be as an investor and probably some kind of advisory assistant to the management. It will give me something to do after I leave Ryanair in around 2009 or 2010. The front of the cabin is where the real money is made and this will be a super-duper product way ahead of anything that Aer Lingus or British Airways has to offer.'

'Somebody at some stage is going to do a long-haul, low-cost airline. Will it be successful? I doubt it.'

'I don't look back at all. I'm 47 and I'm not going to be sitting here pulling wool out of my navel wishing I had done something differently. This is the most fun you can have with your clothes on. There's a danger that I'll self combust.'

'Running Ryanair is sort of an all-consuming activity. I don't have a lot of time for walking around looking at other business opportunities.'

'It would be very difficult for me to don a tie and go onto committees. Could you imagine me looking for a knighthood? Puke. The weakness of British Airways is that everyone is looking for a knighthood.'

'I don't think I'd be capable of setting up Ryanair. I'm not sure I'd be capable of doing any other job you gave me to do, either.'

'I'll be making the world a better place... by taking a vow of silence.'

'Rumours of my demise have been greatly exaggerated.'

'I'll never stop. Better to wear away than to rust away. I like work—it's like a holiday.'

'When the industry is as exciting and interesting as this, I would be crazy to go anywhere else.'

'My scenario here is that I'll be gone out of here in 12 months' time. That's been the plan every year since 1988, and it's the only thing that keeps me sane.'

'I was ready to step down a year ago because it was getting boring, but now everyone says we're in the shit, so I'm definitely staying.'

'I have no intention of hanging around the corridors like Banquo's ghost. The best companies that have survived over the long term are those that have been able to shoot the old guys—old guys go, not get promoted.'

'The last count I did I was 43 years old and I realise I am old for an airline executive today, but no, I am not going anywhere.'

'I'm going in the next two or three years, though that tends to be a bit of a rolling date.'

'I won't be gone in three or five years' time. But I have promised my wife that I will be.'

'I think I'll stay at least another 10 years. I plan to go on and on and on like Chairman Mao.'

'My plan has always been remarkably consistent. I intend to step down in the next two or three years. It's a bit of a movable feast but one day I'll be right.'

'You have to remember that I said I would retire in 1992, that I would retire in 1995, and I think again in 1998. Some of my forecasts have not turned out to be terribly accurate.'

'I suspect this will probably be the last three- or four-year extension I do.'

'They'll find somebody else equally humble, shy and retiring but maybe not as good looking.'

'My eulogy will probably begin with, "He was a jumped-up little bollox" and hopefully will end with, "He lived fast and died young."'

**THE AUTHOR WELCOMES
FEEDBACK FROM READERS.**

PAULKILDUFF@EIRCOM.NET

OR VISIT

HTTP://WWW.PAULKILDUFF.COM

Stung by a ten-hour delay and a €300 fare to Spain on his native 'low-fares' airline, Dubliner Paul Kilduff plots revenge – to fly to every country in Europe for the same total outlay, suffering every low-fares airline indignity. Armed with no more than 10kg of carry-on baggage, he endures 6.00am departures, Six Nations-style boarding scrums, lengthy bus excursions, terminal anxiety and cabin crew who deliver famed customer service.

On his pan-European exploration he reveals the secrets of the new travel phenomenon favoured by one hundred million passengers annually. And his advice to fellow travellers in what is perhaps the ultimate airport holiday read? 'Don't get mad, get even – get a one cent airline ticket!'

NUMBER 1 BESTSELLER *RUINAIR* IS AVAILABLE IN BOOKSHOPS NATIONWIDE FOR ONLY €0.01*

*price excludes fees and charges of €12.98